Family Dog Fusion

A Book to Demystify Your Dog's Behavior So You Can Get the Very Best from Your Dog Training!

By

Bennie Copeland

Owner, Club Canine of Nashville

Co-Founder, FamilyDogFusion.com

Co-Host, Discover Your Dog Podcast

This book is dedicated to **Molly**

When I started getting serious about completing this book, Molly, a mixed Flat-Coated Retriever who I consider to be first dog that was truly mine, was already over 15 years old. She had her good days and her rough days.

Molly passed away in mid-August of 2016, and I used her life as an inspiration to finish it. Molly taught me everything I know about dog training. She was patient, gentle, and willing. She loved me. Because of that love, I was able to learn from her, and I believe she is the reason why I teach the way I do now. Molly endured a lot of ignorance from me. I know she loved me, and I know she wanted to be only with me, but it took a lot to get that through my thick skull.

Molly was the epitome of the social dog. In her younger days, and when she was my only dog, she went everywhere with me. She was never singled out, and she was never that dog that someone went out of their way to say how pretty she was or to comment on her breed. Whenever she was visiting a friend with me, going to an event, or just hanging out at the park, she was just part of me, and I was part of her. Our relationship, the way we blended together, is the reason I named this book Family Dog Fusion.

Lastly, Molly loved people, especially children. I never worried about her when she was around a little baby or even a small child. When she saw a child, she smiled. Literally, she smiled. If you have ever seen a dog smile, you understand what I mean.

She did her job here, she did it well, and I am so much better as a person and trainer for it.

I love you & I miss you, my Molly.

Table of Contents

Forward — vii

Introduction — 1
- How Did I Get Here? — 1
- Why Write This Book? — 7
- Why Do I Train the Way I Do? — 9
- Why Do I Think I Get It? — 16
- What Makes Me Good at What I Do? — 17
- The Purpose of This Book? — 20

Pre-Training Information — 22

Chapter 1
The Three Tools for Training:
Praise, Motivate, Correct — 27
- Praise — 29
  - Speaking in the Affirmative — 40
  - Touch — 45
- Motivate — 47

Motivation as a Method of Training	48
Correct	50
Proper Use of the Leash in Training	51
The Rule of No	52
Correction as a Method of Training	54

Chapter 2

Demystifying Behavior	59
Consistency is the Key	60
Learning What You Are Communicating	62
What Creates Consistency?	63
Controlling Your Energy	64
Understanding the Hierarchy	69
How Dogs vs Humans View the Hierarchy	69
Appropriate Actions and Reactions	73

Chapter 3

Training Progression	76
Getting Started	76
What First?	78
Beginning Your Relationship	79
A Breakdown of the Basic Commands	82
Sit	82

Heel	86
Come	88
Down	90
Place	96

Chapter 4
Making the Commands Work for You — 99

What Are You Communicating?	99
Ten Times in a Row	104
Distractions in Threes	105
Using Distractions with a Purpose	108
Daily Workouts	110

Chapter 5
Being on Purpose with Training — 114

Leave the Leash on Your Dog!	114
Timing of Correction and Praise	116
Correcting After the Fact	117
Anticipation and Avoidance Training	118
Correcting with a Purpose	121
Timing Your Praise	123
Control	125
Using the "All-Done" Command	127

What Your Dog Knows	128
Casual vs Formal Commands	131
Behaviors to Stop vs Behaviors to Never Do	133
Starting the Off-Leash Process	136
The Three Stages for Off-Leash Training	137
Three Rules of Consistency	140
Motivation	144
Correction	145
Success	147
In Conclusion	149
FDF Rules	151
FDF Definitions	154
FDF Postulates	155

Forward

One of the highest honors we can have in our life is to "own" a dog. But this truly begs the question, who "owns" whom? The trust and faithfulness of the companionship of a dog cannot be replicated by anyone or anything else in this world.

Many of us were blessed to have a dog as a child. Someone, if not us, trained that precious animal to sit, stay, go outside to 'empty', or even roll over. We have considered ourselves dog trainers when our pets accomplished these feats – no matter how we were able to encourage them to do so. Agreed, these pets were trained but what about the next steps? Pardon the analogy but, simply because we attend school does not make us an authority on education, and simply because we were somehow able to teach a dog to sit or stay, does not make us an authority on training our precious dogs. This book will completely change your paradigm, if you follow these recommendations of dog training and follow them exactly, you will quickly discover who really needs to be trained.

A few years ago, my husband was working on the back yard and saw a flash, of what he said was either a bobcat or a REALLY fast cat in our backyard. We live in a rather rural area and, on occasion have had various animals abandoned in our area. After much coaxing and encouragement with food underneath a large trailer, we discovered this bobcat was actually a Pitbull puppy covered in ticks, fleas, hungry, and completely destitute. We tried everything we knew, from our early days of dog training – yep, we were dog trainers because we had dogs and trained them – but to no avail. Nothing we tried worked for the long-term.

Isaac would do the things we expected and then, with no warning, go rogue again. We contacted Bennie, who we affectionately refer to as our "Dog Whisperer" and the magic began. He explained to us that the precious honor that we have to "own" a dog quickly transfers the responsibility from the dog to us. We are the caretakers. We are the encouragers. We are the one that our precious responsibility wants to please – not the other way around.

When we realize, as you will throughout this book, that our precious responsibility wants to please us, you will begin to understand how priceless this relationship and responsibility truly is. Go forth and love your pet, just remember who really wants to please whom!

Bill & Denise Pridemore

Former K-9 Officer,

Nashville City Councilman

Introduction

HOW DID I GET HERE?

I have had dogs almost all of my life. I can't remember a time in my childhood that my family didn't have at least one dog. My father loved dogs and wanted to have one, so I never even needed to beg for a dog. At the time, though, the dogs we owned were just that; dogs we owned. We took care of them, fed them, and played with them at times, but mostly they stayed in a pen or in the back yard. I have great memories of some dogs and some I barely recall at all. I remember most of their names and, for the most part, that is all I remember about them unless the dog happened to be there for some major event.

My first dog was Sunny, a Rhodesian Ridgeback. When he was a puppy, I remember him being in my room and running under my bed. We lived in Maryland at the time and had a nice back yard for him. He was smart and incredibly strong, as Ridgebacks were bred to hunt lions. Sunny used his smarts to escape the back yard so often that my father finally had to get a pen for him. I'm not sure if we were moving and had to get rid of him or if he just got to be too much, but at some point, my parents found him another home.

Not until I was married did I have a dog that lived in the house as a part of the family. My wife decided she wanted a lap dog. We went to a dog store, found a little Yorkshire Terrier puppy, and fell in love instantly. He was so tiny he could fit in the palm of my hand. He was somewhere between six to eight weeks old and no more than a few ounces. He was the runt of the litter, and we just loved him. We threw around a few names, but couldn't decide on one until we had him at the house. I was sitting on the floor as he wandered around and I said, "Come here, Berkley!" He turned and flew into my lap and from that point on, his name was Berkley Alexander Copeland.

Berkley was a great dog, and we loved him very much. Our experience in living with Berkley helps explain why I got into the business. I still use him as an example of what not to do when raising and training a dog. The one thing I say over and over to new clients (especially owners of Yorkshire Terriers) is that I may have been bigger than him and he respected me for that, but I was never the boss or owner; he owned me. He was the one that was dominant and in control, and he taught me what dominance truly means.

Berkley was a loving dog and a fantastic part of our family. As long as we did what he wanted, things were great, but there were struggles. We never, in the 13 years he was alive, managed to potty train him. He would always steal underwear or socks and take them to his hideout under the bed. He rarely came when called, and seemed to think "come" meant, "Sit down, I'm coming to get you!" If he was mad at any of us, he'd ignore us and look away when we talked to him. We thought it was amusing at the time, but little did I know, all this time, he was training me, not the other way around. At his biggest, he weighed six pounds, though he weighed about four pounds most of his life. He had a sensitive stomach and couldn't handle human food, and he had to be on a prescription diet most of his adult life. The only thing he could handle was Pizza Bones, our name for the uneaten crusts. It didn't matter if I made the pizza, cooked a frozen pizza, or had pizza delivered, he was there for the bones. Otherwise, he never begged at the table.

As I said before, Berkley never was potty trained. He did learn not to go in front of us, and he would poop and pee outside when we took him. If he had to go when he was in the house, he found places away from us and did his business. We would find the evidence days, sometimes weeks, later. Sometimes it took a while because he would pee many times in the same area, and we only noticed when we started to smell it. I used all the tactics I knew at the time to potty train him. I would take him to the spot, put his nose in it, and spank him, but that would only result in him finding a new place to go. I tried blocking the area so he couldn't get to that spot, but soon we would tire of climbing over the gate or opening a door every time we wanted to pass through and we removed the barrier, resulting in the same actions from Berkley as before.

He was very good at waiting for an opportunity. Since we were gone most of the time during the day, he had free roam of the house. He would never go in our bedroom or the kitchen, probably because these were the places he spent the most time. He would sometimes go in my daughter's bedroom, but that was very rare. For 13 years, we never got him to understand that we wanted him to potty outside. And, in his defense, we never took the time to teach him appropriately what we wanted.

Although there were traits of Berkley's I didn't like, there were many more traits I loved. He loved people, and we never had issues if we took him somewhere, or people came over to the house. He was very social. He was not afraid of other dogs, and for most of his life, he tolerated any dog that was around. As a family, we loved him very much, and he loved us.

When Berkley was ten, we got Gabby. From the time my daughter was eight years old, she asked for a dog of her own. For a couple of years, she asked for a dog for Christmas or her birthday, and we told her that we would not get a dog until we put a fence around the yard. When she was ten, she asked for a fence as a Christmas present. We were sunk. We never planned on fencing in the yard, and now we were held to our promise of getting a dog. So, as a family, we promised to get her a dog on her birthday in the spring, because winter is a tough time to work with and potty train a dog. We also agreed that if we did get her a dog, we would get professional training for the new puppy. At that time, there were few training clubs in the area and the stores offered limited classes.

While looking through the local paper, we found an ad for Border Collie Puppies. The breeder was on the way for a trip we were taking to Kentucky. We called and made an appointment to stop by the breeder's farm to take a look at some of the puppies he had advertised for sale.

When we arrived, we were met by Mike McElya and found out that he only bred Border Collies. Mike is a well-known breeder and takes very good care of his dogs. The dogs he did not sell as puppies he would keep and train to be herding dogs. While we were there, he even showed us how some of the dogs work. Looking back on this event, I now know why Gabby had drive, determination, and intelligence. It was bred into her.

We picked a dog and told Mike that we would pick her up on our way back home. While in Kentucky, we did a little research. From the information we got from Mike and the research we did, we understood that Border Collies were very intelligent and did not make good pets. Mike had even said it would be like constantly having a four-year-old running around the house. I just blew off the information thinking I could handle this dog. As it turned out, the joke was on me.

Gabby was a runt. She was smaller than the rest of the dogs in her litter, and she was a smooth coat. At full size, she never got over 30 pounds, though the average for the Border Collie is 40 to 45 pounds with a curly coat. Being the dog expert I **thought** I was at the time, I just knew that I would be able to handle this runt of a dog. I learned early on that I was wrong.

Gabby was very intelligent. This became apparent early on, and because I was not prepared for this, my methods for training were way off. Later in this book, I will be talking about these methods and my progress from what I thought then to what I believe and teach now. At this time of my life, I was very heavy handed and believed I could scare her into doing what I thought was right. This did not work with Gabby. As a matter of fact, it was detrimental to her character and only created a lot of tension between us early on in her life.

Needless to say, we did not follow through with the training like we said we would, but one day when Gabby was about 12 weeks old, something happened to change our minds. Early one Sunday morning, our neighbor Mrs. Cantrell, a kind older lady, came over to ask something of us. I was outside throwing the ball for Gabby, and the ground was damp from the rain we had the evening before. When Mrs. Cantrell came into the yard, Gabby recognized her and ran to greet her, jumping up and leaving a muddy paw print on her white slacks. I yelled at Gabby, grabbed her by her scruff and threw her inside the house. I was mortified and apologized over and over for Gabby's behavior and for making her late for church.

At that point, I vowed to get a trainer and teach Gabby to never jump on anyone again. I also realized I could not do this on my own, because we had worked on this, and it seemed no matter how much yelling or screaming I did, Gabby still had a tendency to behave in ways I hated. This was going to get fixed!

This was my first time even thinking to hire someone to help me. I felt I should be able to do this on my own and correct these behaviors myself. I don't even remember how we found the trainer, I just know we wanted someone to come to our home and work with us to teach Gabby how to behave.

At the time, our veterinarian did not recommend dog trainers to his clients. It was his thought that owners should be responsible and be able to work on the dog's behaviors themselves. Looking back, I realize that as an owner, the responsible thing to do is know how to communicate appropriately. Had I listened to my vet at the time, I would have done everything I thought worked and would have kept up the same backwards cycle I had understood at the time. Gabby's personality would have been so different than what it is today. As I said earlier, because of my heavy-handed way of training and her intelligence, we started off on the wrong paw, and we were both bound and determined to get our way.

Hiring a trainer, especially one that had a true love and compassion for dogs, was the best thing I could have done to improve our relationship. I remember thinking, after the basic training was complete, how simple the program was. Now, I hear that same reaction from owners that I teach and train many times. This is why I know I am in the right profession. Even now, when I look back at what I learned during those training sessions, if I had not taken the time to bridge the communication gap I was having I would never have been able to have the relationship with dogs the way I do now. As simple as it seemed at the time, if there had not been someone willing to take the time to teach me, I would have stayed on the same path I grew up with, and I would have ended up with that same dog in the back yard that I always had growing up.

WHY WRITE THIS BOOK?

In the last 15+ years, I have learned a lot. Mainly, I realized I am good at explaining what I have learned. I have been sharing that information over the years to a small, select group of people that hire me to train their personal dogs. With this book, not only do I get to share how to communicate with your dog more effectively, I also get to reach a bigger audience of dog lovers.

I began to examine how I was helping others and listening to what they said about me to their friends and colleagues as well. Most of the time, my clients want to give me the credit for training their dog and yet, they did the work. I just taught them how to communicate with their dog. This proper communication helped them to fix the problems or learn to respond to their dog appropriately in every given situation. Through this book, I hope to share that same knowledge and help others find the joy in communicating with their dogs.

I say that Molly, my Retriever, was truly *my* first dog. Berkley was bought because Kate wanted a dog, Gabby was bought because Jessica wanted a dog, but Molly found me! I have had dogs all my life, but they were not a part of my life like Molly was. Now I'm in the process of creating this bond with Oz, an Australian Cattle Dog that I took in from a no-kill shelter.

Oz was considered "unadoptable" because of his aggression toward other dogs. I looked at how he behaved around people, and I saw an incredible dog. His personality was very different than Gabby's or Molly's, and he had to be handled differently as well.

When I started working with him, I noticed he could get along with other dogs if he was introduced properly. After working with him for a very short time, I introduced him to my dog, Molly, and they were compatible; they became the very best of friends. He now has many dog friends because I work with him on a daily basis, especially when it comes to meeting a new dog.

Part of what has made me successful is that my body language to a dog is totally open. I adjust my attitude to meet the dog's needs, and let them see it. For a dog that is friendly and outgoing, this is awesome! They know I am going to be friendly with them as well. In a matter of minutes, the dog has calmed down. This sometimes upsets an owner because the dog does not show the bad behaviors they wanted me to help fix.

For a dog that is timid or anxious, I can be comforting. Most of the time, the dog will warm up to me very quickly. This also frustrates the owner, especially if their dog is not warming up to one of the family members.

For a dog that is dominant or aggressive, I am very intimidating, almost threatening. I have had owners in this situation that have told me that their dog has never treated anyone the way it treated me (growling or sometimes fearful). This gets tricky, because in the owner's mind, it looks like the dog is making a judgment about me and because the dog does not like me immediately, I am the bad guy. I used to think this, too, but now, I realize that because of my demeanor, I am threatening the dog's dominance. I am intimidating just by my confidence and my presence. I meet very few dogs with this type of behavior because true dominance is not a common trait in a dog. When I do get a truly dominant dog, I have to really assess the owner's ability to comprehend the training and their willingness to do the work. Because and owner does not see these traits in a dog like I can, it can be a very long and difficult process to teach the owner and train the dog.

WHY DO I TRAIN THE WAY I DO?

Along the way, I have learned many things that influenced me to use the methods I train with now.

It started with the training I paid for with Gabby. I interviewed the owner of Cumberland Canine to come to my home and train me.

Two things stood out for me. I liked the way he talked about training, and I liked him personally. My mindset was very different than it is now, and I liked how he talked about being in control and teaching our dog to be a great part of the family. I told him that I wanted to do the program, and he said he would have a trainer call us and set up times to do the weekly sessions. At first, I was put off by this. Here he was telling me about everything he would teach me, but he was going to send out someone else to do our training. Then, I met our personal trainer, Judy. I loved her instantly. She was very down to earth and practical. Judy was up front with us from the beginning and did not sugarcoat the training once we got started.

Judy did a great job working with our family. Jessica and I did the bulk of training, and we loved it so much that we went beyond the basic obedience we were learning at home with Gabby. We participated in many festivals, we travelled, and competed in agility trials. We participated and conducted classes and seminars about training and behavior, and we did many other activities that were outside the normal family/dog relationship. Judy played a big part by encouraging us and participating in these activities with us.

There are a few things that stand out for me during my training process with Gabby. One is that when we were training Gabby, there would be times that Judy would tell me do something a certain way but could not explain why. When I would do it the way she told me, it worked, yet I did not know why, and this drove me crazy. At one point, I decided I was not going to do it the way she told me and the training became very difficult. I refused to do it the way she said if she couldn't explain the reason I should do it that way. It became so bad that at one point she told me not to work Gabby for a week. This killed me. Gabby and I were going through some major dominance issues, and I was going to win, no matter what.

The fact that Judy could not explain why a certain process worked was a big frustration to me. When I am working with a client now I get asked why I am telling them to do a particular thing, and I feel it is very important to explain the purpose of my instructions. While working with Judy, what I did understand at that time was that correction worked. This was my training mentality and one of the reasons I liked the style of training I was being taught at that time, even though I did not understand the whys.

I thought the training seemed easy, something I could do myself. Yes, there were pitfalls and there were some rough times between Gabby and I, but when it was all over, I could not believe I had to pay someone $700 to teach me to train a dog.

I loved doing the training so much that I approached Jim and Tammy from Cumberland Canine about working for them part-time. At this time, I owned my own business and made my own hours. They said yes, and I started working for them at their kennel. I worked for them for about a year part-time, and then about another year full-time. It was a great experience overall. This was the true foundation of my education in a dog's behavior, personality and capacity to learn. I was thrown right into working with dogs all day long. One of the big things I learned is that like humans, all dogs are different in all aspects. When you couple these traits with all of the different traits of people, it really can complicate things.

When I worked for Cumberland Canine, I learned a tremendous amount about dogs. On slow weeks, I was working with two to four dogs, and during the busy seasons, I worked with more than 50 dogs on a daily basis. I fed, exercised, trained, and socialized with these dogs from four to 12 hours a day. It is very difficult to put into words how much I learned with so many different dogs in such a short time period. Cumberland Canine did not just work with easy dogs with great personalities; they took in aggressive dogs, dogs with huge fears and anxieties, dogs that had horrendous backgrounds, as well as dogs that came from great and loving backgrounds. We worked with purebred dogs as well as mixed breed and the so-called "designer breeds." No dog was too small or too large; no dog was too aggressive or too nice. There were very few reasons to ever reject a dog from training. I do not recall Jim or Tammy ever turning down a dog to train, though I do recall turning down a few owners. I would say that I worked with hundreds of dogs during my two years with Cumberland Canine. During that time, I was exposed to almost every range of dog you can imagine. There are many breeds out there I still have not had the honor of working with, but there is not a dog out there I would ever think I could not work with because of my experience and what I learned at Cumberland Canine.

Yet, I found myself driving to work, wondering why I hated my job. After about a year and a half, I was done. I did not like going to work with the dogs, and I did not like going to work with the people there.

I did some real soul searching about my job, and I was totally floored as to why I did not love my job anymore. I loved the dogs! I still do and to this day I love working with every dog I come into contact with, whether it be on a walk or going into a potential client's home. I love dogs. What I didn't like was the method of training I had learned. Instead of giving up on dog training, I took what truly worked for all dogs from the methods I had learned and what experience taught me, and I formed my own training method, which I still use today.

I was taught to train by using fear. Our goal was to break the dog down, then build her back up. This was said to me so many times that I still, to this day, hear the voice of my teacher, and mentor at the time, saying this when I write it. Living this kind of life soon becomes very miserable for humans. You can only imagine what it must do to a dog. It was painful for me to realize this, because I bought into it. I thought this was how it was supposed to be done. I thought I was doing what should be done in order to teach a dog because this is how I was living my personal life as well.

One of the things I was taught was that if a dog broke its command, you should correct the dog until it was back in command. In other words, if a dog was in a down and it got up, I was to continue giving corrections to the dog until it lay back down. The longer it continued to stand or sit, the tougher the corrections would become. When I was practicing with Molly, it was usually outside and she would run away as far as the neighbor's yard. I would correct her all the way back to the spot where she was to lay down. The next time she broke the command, it was a yard or two further in the neighborhood before I could catch her. I would catch her and correct her back. The next time it would be harder and longer. It got to the point that when she saw me coming, she would run. When she broke the command, she would see me and run. I was chasing her for blocks--one time, over a mile! She was running through the neighborhood, terrified of me catching her because she knew the result. I was pissed off, and she was scared.

One day, after chasing Molly through the neighborhood again, I just lost it. I was so frustrated that she would not stay in command for me that when I finally got within about 20 feet of her I sat down, and started crying. I looked up at her, scared, and just said; "If you don't want to stay with me, then go." I stayed where I was for a while and coaxed her to come near me. When she finally did, I took off the leash and her collar, and I told her she could go. I thought to myself, if she is so miserable with me, then she should find another family to stay with. I loved on her for a long time, then I got up and started walking home. She followed. We got about halfway home, and I noticed that she, again, was sniffing around just like she always did. Her nose always seemed to be the thing that got her in trouble. It was something I was never able to break her of, sniffing new and old smells. When I noticed she was not paying attention, I sat down again. I waited and watched her for a few moments then I called her to me. She came, a little more willing this time. Once again, I headed home and she followed, almost all the way to the house. For the rest of the day, she and I stayed in the yard. I would sit down and call her to me every now and then, and she started coming to me without hesitation. Over the next few months, I noticed her breaking her commands less and less, and being very attentive when I gave a command, even when her nose was buried in some great smell.

This was my very first lesson in using praise as a method of training. I thought I was doing that in the past, but this incident made me realize I wasn't. This was not the only realization, nor was it the entire reason I now train and teach the way I do. This was what I look back on and recognize as the beginning of the process through which I was to make the change in my training methods.

Another defining moment for me was a puppy named Savannah. She was a boxer puppy and very sweet. Her owner did not want to do the training, so she sent her to Cumberland Canine to do the 30-day training program. Throughout my time at Cumberland Canine I was being taught how to train dogs, yet no one ever taught me to look for the differences in a dog's personality and adjust my training accordingly. I was just teaching the dog the commands using the tools I knew.

15

This became a problem with Savannah. She did not like the leash. When I brought this up to the owners, their advice was to just drag her around and correct her until she was compliant. So, I did just that. I would drag her for great lengths around the training room thinking I was motivating her to want to walk on a leash. Eventually she would walk with me on the leash and eventually she would do all of the commands, only with her head bowed way down low, as if she was totally dreading the leash, the walks, and the commands. The curious thing was, when she was off the leash, she was so fun, exciting, and lively. The moment the leash went on her collar, she bowed that head and went into the dreaded work mode.

I did not understand at the time what I was doing to her and the misery I was enforcing on her, because her personality was very sweet. She was not a dog that needed correction at all. I have compared this in the past with children. There are some children you can just look at funny, and they will cringe and comply.

Then there are those kids that need a knock on the head (just an expression!) to get them to even pay attention. Savannah was not the "knock-on-the-head" dog. This was extremely evident once that leash was off. She would do anything until I gave a command. Then she would just stop in her tracks and bow her head. I started working with her off the leash to see if I could make the commands fun for her, and it worked. We had fun playing with each other and eventually she even enjoyed doing the commands, only off-leash. Even when she was doing all of the commands excitedly, if I was to put that leash on, she went back to the sad, puppy look. What I did not realize then is what the leash represented. The harsh way she was trained broke her of ever wanting to be leashed.

I did not realize how I had incorporated this into my own training style until years later when I owned my own kennel. My employees would question my contradictions when training different dogs. They would say, "One day you tell us do something a certain way, then the next day you tell us not to do that thing you said to do before." When teaching the basic commands, there are basic techniques that will stay the same with all dogs. However, what I hadn't put into words until then was that the levels of Praise, Motivation, and Correction must be adjusted to fit the dog's personality. I was making these adjustments without realizing what I was doing. When I taught an owner (or my employees), I was teaching based on what I knew about that dog's personality without explaining that it has to be different with each dog, because they are only dealing with that one dog at that time.

WHY DO I THINK I GET IT?

The answer here is both simple to answer and difficult to explain. First, I understand the hierarchy of dogs. Second, I understand how to make a dog feel very comfortable when I am around, without even trying. When working with a new dog, a client will sometimes comment on how well their dog behaves for me and not for them. My quick explanation is that I have been doing this for over 15 years and have a lot of practice. Because of this practice, I make things look very easy and often the dog will work better for me than the owner. I always expect the dog to do what I say. In the home environment, owners are very inconsistent. They 'pick their battles' and this creates a chance for the dog to continue to test the boundaries with them.

Owners, including myself, have a tendency to be inconsistent throughout their normal everyday life. My dogs know when I am serious and when I am not, just like my daughter knew growing up. In my own personal life, I create boundaries and I choose my battles, just like everyone else. Sometimes I am very willing to stick with the rules, and sometimes I bend them. Bending the rules is normal, and it is inconsistent. Consistency, however, is vital during the training process.

Also, I have done the work. I have over 40 years of being with and observing dogs. There were times I would just sit in crowded dog parks for hours watching dogs interact with dogs, children, and owners. I have trained dogs to do skilled activities such as agility and high-level obedience. I have read so many books, it is mind-boggling, and I have trained many different people with many different personalities. My training method is an accumulation of everything I have done every day of my life involved with dogs.

WHAT MAKES ME GOOD AT WHAT I DO?

I was on a website for a boarding kennel that offers facility training in my home town and saw this huge list of all the classes, training certifications, and past experiences of the owner. This trainer offered 14-day and 21-day training courses. I looked at all of those certifications and just shook my head. I have seen the results and heard the horror stories about the dogs this person has trained. I have also been a part of the travesties this boarding kennel has created. On more than one occasion I have had to retrain the dog (or owner). I would never want to be associated with this kennel, let alone let them take my dog for any amount of time and yet, people see all of those letters behind the name and the long lists of certifications and think this guy is a great trainer because of the list of accomplishments.

I have seen how this person's business works first-hand, and I know they absolutely care nothing about the client or the dogs. It is very sad. I mention it because it does not matter what the person's training background is. It does not matter if someone has completed so many courses or passed so many tests, nor does it matter what accomplishments someone has had if there is no love for the job, if there is no respect for a living creature (person or animal), and if there is no joy in the work. You can be the most decorated trainer around and you will still have appalling results.

I love what I do and it shows in the results.

I love to teach someone to create an awesome part of the family. I love to be in front of people. I have always known that I would be a teacher in some way. I have managed multi-million-dollar companies, I have started numerous businesses and I have created clubs, business network groups, and personal development groups and yet, I always come back to the basics. Teaching gives me great pleasure. I love working with adults and children alike. I have been doing some sort of teaching or coaching almost all of my adult life and I look back on those times as the most memorable.

I am good at it, too. I have a knack for getting it when someone has not fully understood what I was talking about and I can shift to explain it in a different way that helps them understand. I look at it as a personal responsibility to make sure an owner understands what to do in any given situation, and I work on it until they do. I never tell an owner that they did something wrong during a lesson, I tell them I did not explain it correctly. I take responsibility.

I get it and that's it! I understand dogs and families, and I know how to fuse the two together.

A friend and I were walking through her neighborhood. We walked past some people that were yelling for their dog that had run off. When we got close enough to them, she asked me, "Why is it that some dogs will run off and your dog, Oz, always wants to stay around?"

I responded to her with a question of my own: "Why do you think your children want to stay around you?" This comparison is very interesting to me. It explains a few things about family relationships and the difference between how dogs learn and how children learn. This is the foundation of what my training is all about.

If your dog trusts that you are going to act in a certain way, no matter what the situation is, she will always want to be with you (unless the way you act is extremely negative). If you are more consistent in praising your dog for making your desired choice, your dog will test the boundaries less, your bond will become stronger, and your dog will want to stay with you more. This does not mean there will not be distractions that tempt your dog; this just means there is a desire to be with the people she trusts the most. This trust and love can only be created by you. It comes down to the two basic things that are the theme of this entire book and my training strategy: Structure and Consistency.

THE PURPOSE OF THIS BOOK

The purpose for me writing this book is multi-layered. Over the years I have come up with rules and theories about dog training that I know work, thanks to constant testing and tweaking. I have seen many of these rules and postulates proven and reinforced by other trainers, teachers, and researchers, but I've never seen them put together like you will see here.

Most of the rules here are for the people, not the dog. Why? Because I train people, not dogs. Dogs, in general, behave the same way no matter what the breed or size because they are reactive. Dogs do not analyze each situation like humans do . . . and dogs can't read. This book would not be very effective if I expected them to read it! Most people do not understand how dogs learn or how to communicate with their dog. Through this process, I am teaching you to respond to your dog, in accordance to your dog's ability, personality, and intelligence. I'm also working with you, the owner, according to your ability, personality, and intelligence.

Understanding this process is easy. It is the practice that is difficult. Owners tend to be impatient, unwilling to change how they communicate, and unwilling to put in the time, practice, and repetition needed for teaching a certain behavior.

I was an adult when I started this process in 2001. I was 35 years old. I have had dogs all of my life, and before Gabby, I never would have thought to hire a trainer to teach me. If it was not for my daughter's desire to have a dog, I would not be living my dream of being a dog trainer. I would not be writing this book and maybe not even have two dogs lying at my feet while I am writing. I understand, especially when an owner gets a good dog, the feeling that there is no reason for training. That was my attitude for a long time. And yet, if you have a great new member of the family, why would you not take the time to learn how to communicate with them?

PRE-TRAINING INFORMATION

Chapter One of this book is the most challenging and most important part. I will constantly refer to chapter one. In this part of the book, you will learn more about dog communication if, and when, you decide to take on training. This section is the basis for what I do. You will understand how to communicate with your dog and the most important aspects of having a pet. Take your time in this chapter; read it more than once. Refer back to it often.

The most important thing you will learn is how to get what you want and expect from your dog. Even though it sounds simple enough, most of you do not understand this concept as it pertains to dog/human communication. In order to start this path toward understanding what you want, you have to first know what the word *Praise* really means when it comes to training your dog. Once I understood what praise meant and how to express what I wanted from my dogs, my whole life changed and continues to change every day. How I train now is a result of understanding this concept and being able to explain it to you.

There are a few things you need to know before diving into this book. Whether I take a dog into my facility to train, work with a new trainer to learn about dog training and behavior, or work with an owner in their home, these are the basic rules and theories I use and teach. The rules and theories can be applied in every situation. How they are applied depends on the dog's personality, the trainer/owner's personality, and the level of willingness to train and be trained.

The goal here is to have fun. Enjoy working with your dog and she will enjoy working with you. By using this guide, you will learn to enjoy the time spent with your dog and she will look forward to your sessions together. What you are really learning is how to communicate appropriately with your dog.

[Note: I keep referring to your dog as a "she." The dogs I started training with, Molly and Gabby, were females. I give many examples using both of them. They are very different in levels of intelligence and desire to work. This is okay, and these examples will let you see how my training techniques will work with any dog, regardless of gender or breed, with any drive and intellect.]

Learning to keep a steady tone and calm, easygoing body language is the biggest challenge for most of you. When working with your dog, you will have to keep it together. Yelling, screaming, frustration, and punishment have no place in training. Leave that for the interstate at rush hour. Enjoy the time you spend with your dog. If you look forward to the lessons, so will she. Come up with a catchy phrase or word that you can use when you are starting to do the training. I hear people say, "Let's work" or "Okay, it's time to work" all the time. That's great. Say it in a positive and upbeat manner. I would like to hear people say "Hey, let's play!" This way, it doesn't sound like a chore. Keep it snappy, upbeat, and fun. "Are you ready to PLAY?"

It is also important to be aware of your energy. Have you ever noticed that when you are hyper and ready to go, your dog is, too? The opposite is true as well. If you are tired or sick, you may see that your dog is relaxed or melancholy. When I get in a writing groove, both of my dogs get very calm and lay down. When I come home from a great day of work, my dogs greet me with excitement and seem very difficult to calm down. This may not always be the case, but being aware of your energy can make a big difference when working with your dog. It's easy to say you should keep a calm, easygoing tone for working, but that is not always easy after a long day of work or a personal workout. The changes in your energy can affect your dog's energy as well.

Energy is an interesting thing. When I trained with the trainers that worked for me, I would go into great detail about how their energy affects their workout and the dog. When they told me about a difficult situation, a problem with a particular dog, or a specific problem behavior, I could hear the frustration in their tone of voice. I also hear that frequently when a potential new client calls about a behavior they want to "fix." In those situations, the trainer/owner has been working with that negative energy, and those emotions are being transferred to the dog.

With my trainers, I ask them to sit still for a few minutes before getting the dog, to tell themselves how great this workout will be, to think about the workout as fun, and to think about why and how they are going enjoy the dog and the workout. They are not allowed to touch the dog until they sit for two or three minutes giving the self-induced pep talk. It always works! Their workout is much better than past sessions with that dog. They almost always get better, if not awesome, results from the dog in that workout.

Who changed in this scenario, the dog or the trainer? Attitude means everything. I have a small sign above my door that I can read every day that says, "The happiest people don't have the best of everything, they just make the best of everything." Taking that short time to create a new attitude and a new view can be the difference between a horrible experience and a good experience. It can also be the difference between a good experience and an awesome experience.

There are times when a client calls and is extremely frustrated with how the training is going. Most of the time, I just tell them to take a break. Stop working the dog for a day or two. When you take the opportunity to enjoy your dog, you are much more likely to want to work with her, and she is much more likely to want to work with you. If you feel the frustration coming on, does this mean you need to stop working every time? No, just take a break! Shift your attitude. The practice comes in catching yourself. Working through the frustration and staying intent on a positive, fun workout is the best way to keep the training moving in the right direction.

If you have picked up this book, it is because you are in for the long haul. You might want to get a jump on training early, or you could have some frustrating behaviors that have shown up in your dog that you want to fix. Either way, you have shown a dedication to your dog that most owners don't. You have decided to do something about it instead of getting rid of the dog or ignoring the issues.

If your goal with this book is to fix the problem or get rid of the dog, you have wasted your money. This is not a quick-fix manual. This is about understanding your dog's behavior and learning how to adjust your communication so you can create a great member of your family. In my podcast, Discover Your Dog, the opening line is "The show that demystifies your dog's behavior so you can get the best results from your dog training." It says, to me, that we are going to clear up those questions, tell you why your dog does the things that drive you crazy, and help you get the best results when you work and train with your dog. Notice that you still have to train. Understanding why is only the beginning of the process, and it is up to you as to how well you want your dog to behave. Yes, you have to do the work.

I worked with certified trainers for over two years before going out on my own. One word of advice was whatever you do with your new dog (be it a puppy, full-grown, or a rescue) for the first 30 days will determine how that dog behaves around you for the rest of its life. I encourage you to take the time and really push through the frustration, stay as consistent as you can, and create a structure that you and your dog can live with. Do it continually for the first one to three months you have your new dog. Also, when you take the time to get it right up front, you can have a happy and enjoyable dog for the rest of its life.

This doesn't mean you're sunk if there's a problem and you've had the dog for a month or more. By learning the practices throughout this book, you can still have a great member of your family. It may take a little longer and require more awareness on your part. You have already established some boundaries; you now have to change your actions to create new and better boundaries.

CHAPTER 1

THE THREE TOOLS FOR TRAINING: PRAISE, MOTIVATE, CORRECT

In the business I am in, I talk, teach, and associate with very busy people. As a professional, I understand that most people want an obedient dog, but they just don't have the time to put in training to get their dog to a high level of obedience. This book will show you how to communicate your needs and expectations in a relatively short time. By putting in one to three short sessions a day, you can train your dog. You will also be learning how to better communicate through these practice sessions. This works! I do not want you to stress yourself out. I don't want your dog to be stressed out. Consistency is the key ingredient, to teach and for your dog to learn from you.

New clients often tell me they are skeptical. They don't believe their dog will do the things I tell them she will learn. Even at the end of the training, they are amazed and in awe of what they have accomplished. These clients are not just professionals, but young people, retired husbands and wives, housewives or househusbands, and yes, even children! Even a child can understand and put into practice my methods. The more people in one household that participate in the training process, the better. Almost every age (walking, talking, and processing information are a must!), any social status, any ability or disability, can adapt and use this program. If you can read this book, you can put your hands on a leash and walk, wheel, or stumble around the room and get started.

Family Dog Fusion is about dog/human behavior. I have developed and compiled my tools, rules, definitions, and postulates so that any person can use and understand these rules when training their dog. When reading this information, you will notice how simple and easy to comprehend most of it is. The work comes in the day-to-day practice. It takes practice. Practice creates awareness, awareness leads to consistency. It all goes back to consistency.

This chapter provides the tools you need to begin training. Other than this book, a leash, and a collar, you do not have to buy any extra gadgets or tools. The tools are all about understanding how to create structure and consistency. If it takes reading the first part of the book a few times before getting started with the training, I would suggest you do that. It may make more sense the second or third time you read it, and you will know where to come back to when you have a question in the midst of training.

In the following chapters, I will cover the basic tools everyone uses when training. Later in the book, I will tie together many other aspects of training that will help you understand these basic tools better. You will also learn what you need to do to go beyond the basics and continue with great communication, even off the leash. Remember, the tools are here for you to reference back to anytime, and you should.

The three tools you will be using are Praise, Motivation, and Correction. As you can probably guess, there is a big difference between praise and correction; The difference between Praise and Motivation, however, is more subtle. These are the tools you will be learning about and learning to use appropriately. Many of my clients confuse praise and motivation. Hopefully, you will truly understand the difference once you have completed this part of the book. This is why I suggest you read it multiple times.

PRAISE

The first and most important tool for training is **Praise**! Praise really is the only *method* to use for training. Why is this? In order to teach and expect obedience, you must first understand what obedience is when it comes to training your dog.

Obedience is defined by Merriam-Webster's Dictionary as the willingness to obey. The only way to get your pet to be "willing to obey" is by using praise. By using anger or coercion, you are only creating a reaction of fear or expectation, not willingness. Praise creates this willingness. Praise is how you get the response you need every time. Teaching your dog by rewarding her with love and happiness creates and attracts love and happiness. Most dogs, and most people, want to please others by nature. When you or your dog knows someone that is pleasing and trustworthy, you both desire to be near that person.

> **Postulate:** Praise is the only way you are truly teaching your dog. It is the only way you are going to get your dog to be willing to do what you want.

Once you understand that praise is the only way you are teaching and training, there are two very important segments you need to know:

1. The only time you are truly teaching your dog is when she is making a choice, and you praise her for making that choice.
2. In any given situation, what choice do you want your dog to make?

This is the breakdown of true communication for you and your dog. Once you really understand and can put into practice these two "Praise Segments," you will be on the road to great communication with your dog. Great communication leads to a better bond, and the better you and your dog bond, the better your dog will fuse into your family.

These two things are now the foundation of my training methods, and I consider them the most important part of this book. I can teach you to understand what you want from your dog. If you want effective communication with your dog, the above two items are, undeniably, the most important things you can learn in this book.

The very first thing you have to ask yourself is why do you want to do this training? Why do you want to put yourself and your dog through a program that could be intense, and why do you want to put in all of this time to train?

If you answered the above question with anything other than "I want to make my dog a great part of the family," then you may want to reconsider what you are doing. There are no guarantees in this book other than this: if you follow the directions and you put in the effort, you will make your dog a great part of your family. What you are doing by choosing this book is learning how to communicate. You are learning how to bridge the communication gap between you and your dog. This book cannot "fix" anything. You are the only one that can do that.

Though dogs are often compared to children, communicating with your dog is much different than communicating with a child. The same basic structure may apply, yet a child makes analytical decisions. A dog only reacts to a certain action during a behavior. This can be as complicated or as simple as you make it. One argument I frequently hear is about a dog being jealous or spiteful. It is not possible for a dog to be jealous or spiteful because these are analytical behaviors. Dogs do not reason or analyze. On some level it may seem they can, or do, reason or analyze. I would argue that when a dog has to make a choice on their own there has to be some judgement made, but in all the time I have been working with dogs and people, I have learned that dogs only react to what they have learned. Like a child that seeks attention, a dog will see what gets your attention then and then repeat those behaviors. Unlike children, whose reactions will change as they learn and analyze their situations, dogs will react the same way each time the same set of circumstances is presented. So, when one of the three tools for training is used on a dog, she will only react to that tool according to the situation.

How are you going to bridge that communication gap? By teaching you the proper tools for training, by showing you when and how to use the tools correctly and by creating structure and consistency with your dog.

Praise Segment 1: *The only time you are teaching your dog is when she is making a choice.*

Whenever your dog is making a choice or has a big reaction, and you give your dog attention for that choice or reaction, this is when you are teaching and communicating what you want. This is where the three tools really come into play.

- If you praise your dog during the choice, you are teaching her to do that thing.
- If you motivate your dog during the choice, she is more likely to remember and want to do that thing.
- If you correct your dog appropriately during the choice, you are teaching her to not do that thing.

Later, we will go into detail about the difference between motivation and praise. For now, what you need to know is that any time you give your dog attention, or have a big reaction to something, while she is making a choice, it is praise. If there is no choice being made, then it is not praise; it is just motivation. It is a complex part of understanding how to work with your dog because too many times, you think you are praising when you are really just motivating. Most of you think that just because you are doing something positive with your dog, you are praising your dog. The word 'praise', in terms of training is just attention. That attention does not have to be positive or negative.

For example, my dogs are not allowed on the furniture. My dogs also roam free in my house when I am gone. When I leave, they are left to their own devices. When I get home, they are usually hanging out on the floor in the living room, or they are greeting me at the door. I always give my dogs lots of love when I walk through the door. At this time, am I teaching them that I want them to stay on the floor? Most times, a new client will say, "Yes." The answer is "no," because they are not making a choice. They are just hanging out on the floor or greeting me at the door. To teach them to learn to stay on the floor, I had to get my dogs to make the choice of whether to get on the couch or to stay on the floor.

Some people do this naturally, without even knowing they are teaching. I hear many people say they want their dog to sit before putting on the leash and going for a walk. After a while, the dog will sit automatically when the owner gets the leash. This is because without even realizing it, the owner starts praising her when she sits. If she doesn't sit, the owner may ignore her or keep the leash away from their dog. The motivation was getting to go outside for a walk.

How do you get your dog to make a choice? Continuing with my example, I put my dog into situations that she could choose. The choice was to either get on the furniture or to stay on the floor. One of the ways I would do this was to put something of temptation such as a toy or treat onto the furniture. If she put her paws on the furniture, I would quickly correct with the leash and say "no." "No" means, "Stop doing what you are doing and pay attention to me." It only needs to be as firm as you need to make your dog stop and pay attention. Then, I would tempt again. Usually, within three to four times, my dog would make the choice to stay on the floor when the toy was on the furniture. The moment she chose to stay on the floor, even with the big temptation of the toy, I would praise her excitedly and give her the toy. This was the choice I wanted. I continued to practice throughout the day and would test her no more than 10 times in a day.

Let's say for example, I corrected my dog six times for jumping up on the couch, on this first day of tests, and I had four praise situations for her making the choice to stay on the floor. Using this one-day example (putting my dog into this situation 10 times), I want to break down the process my dog and I went through. First, the very first time she chose to stay on the floor was out of fear. She feared being corrected again and chose the floor. I never want my dog to fear me for any reason. The intention of the correction is not to hurt my dog; the intention is only to get her to stop doing what she is doing and pay attention to me. If the correction is appropriate, you are giving your dog an opportunity to make another choice. Second, most people will quit working on the choice or behavior after one or two praises. They think their dog has learned what they want because of the few successes they saw and praised for. The problem here is the owner has not even scratched the surface.

I came up with my very first rule in dog training because I never want my dog to fear me, and I realized Molly had not learned that lesson in that one session.

The Ten to One Rule: For every *one* time you correct your dog for anything, you must praise your dog *10* times for doing the thing *you want* in that situation.

This rule can be hard to accept because the moment you catch your dog making a good choice, you think your dog has learned to make that choice every time. Also, when your dog does something good once or twice, you think your dog will make that same choice every time, no matter what the situation.

Why 10 to one? Anything you do once or twice does not create or discourage a behavior. If you have to correct your dog once for a behavior, such as jumping up, you now have to make her approach people 10 times, praising her when she stays on all four legs, and continue to correct her for jumping, if necessary. The 10 to one rule works because you need the practice. You have to practice watching for your dog to make the choice to stay on all four legs when you are approaching. If you catch your dog staying on all fours ten times more than you are correcting her for jumping, you will create a willingness from your dog to stay on all fours.

Another reason to praise ten time more than correct is the fear factor. You don't want your dog to fear you. By practicing praising your dog ten times more that you ever correct, you are creating a behavior your dog will want to do to please you. For most dogs, wanting to please you is in their nature.

During the beginning of this process, it can seem impossible. It may be that you approach that same person four more times after the first correction and only get one praise out of the entire process. Now you have to set up this situation at least 39 more times.

35

Why 39 more times, and do you have to do them right then? In the example, you approached a person five times, corrected four times, and praised once. The 10:1 ratio says you must praise 10 times for every one correction; this equals 40 praises. You got one praise, so you only have to praise 39 more times, just from this short session. And, no, you do not have to do the approaches right then. This would get very tiresome and frustrating.

I suggest you actively work on any one behavior no more than 10 times a day. To correct for that behavior throughout the day (or week) is appropriate. Correcting for a behavior is 24/7. It would also be smart to count how many times you correct for the behavior outside of the times you are working on it. Remember, you have to add 10 more times to work on it for every single time you correct. Yes, **every** time you correct. I also suggest you only work on one behavior at a time. In other words, your dog may be a jumper and a play-biter; to work on both of these at the same time is going to get very frustrating for you and your dog. It can also get very confusing.

After I really understood how important this rule was, I started to realize some interesting things about it. The first thing was that it takes time and effort to reach this goal. It is inevitable that you will catch your dog doing the behavior you don't want at some point, especially if you haven't worked on that behavior for a while.

I remember how bad Molly was about jumping up, and how much I worked on it. She had been doing so well with this behavior that I hadn't worked on it for months. One day, I was at the dog park with her, and she ran up to this couple and jumped on the woman. I was totally caught off guard, and it scared the woman. I yelled, "No!" at Molly as she proceeded to howl and bark at the woman.

Of course, through all my screaming, body language, and frustrated tone, I am sure the woman thought she was going to be bitten. In the moment, I was shocked and had no clue why Molly was doing this. When I reached Molly and got control of my emotions, I told the woman that she rarely barks at anyone and when she does, she generally wants attention or food. I told her that Molly's only barks to get attention. The woman relaxed, and Molly was totally ecstatic that she was getting attention from this woman. I was very surprised at how she was acting.

Looking back, I had separated from my wife about a year before, and Molly had not seen her in a very long time. This woman was about the same build and height, with the same color hair as my wife. This particular dog park was one to which my wife and I frequently took Molly. Thus, I can only imagine that this was the reason Molly acted this way around a complete stranger. This entire story is about the fact that I had relaxed working on the jumping up behavior and in this situation, she was willing to test the boundary.

This brings on an extension of the Ten to One Rule. Your dog will always be willing to test the boundary of any behavior until you have reached a lifetime ratio of praising your dog 10 times more than you have ever corrected your dog for doing that behavior. This takes a very long time and a complete awareness of always praising your dog every time she does what you want.

For example, I praise my dogs every time they potty outside. I have reached the ratio of praising them 10 times more in their lives for doing this outside, and I know it. They never intentionally go to the bathroom in my house. Potty training is an easy one to reach because you intentionally work on that behavior daily, and you are very aware that you want your dog to potty outside. Most other behaviors are not so easy. To hit this lifetime ratio, you have to really be aware of when your dog is making choices, especially when it comes to the behavior you want to work on.

> **Postulate:** When you have hit the lifetime ratio of praising your dog 10 times more than you have ever corrected, your dog will always choose to do the behavior you want, even if you are not there.

I hope you are beginning to see how long this process can be. It truly is a lifetime of communication and consistency. However, it is really up to you. This is where I hope you are learning how important it is to create structure and to be consistent.

> **Postulate:** Structure means rules! By creating and abiding by these rules, you will always be doing the same things and always expecting the same results.

When I started training other people as well as dogs, I needed some way to explain how to employ consistency to others. I came up with that ratio and the Ten to One Rule. This was something that made sense to me; I could apply it to training dogs, and I could explain why it works to a dog owner.

Along with the Ten to One Rule, another rule needs to be applied when using this ratio of praise to correction.

> **Rule of Praise - Part 1:** Praise must always be at a much higher level than the level of your correction.

In other words, the correction may have been a slight pull with a simply stated "no" or it may have been a much firmer pull with a very firm "NO." Either way, once the correction has worked and you get the result you were looking for, you have to praise at a much higher level than you corrected.

Praise Segment 2: *Once you really understand segment one—that your dog has to be making a choice—then the second part of the tool of praise comes into play: What is the choice?*

In any given situation, what choice do you want your dog to make? This begins to get very complicated, because everyone wants something different. Some people are okay with their dog being on the furniture, some are not. Some people are willing to let their dog jump up, some don't. What I perceive as good behavior, someone else may think is atrocious behavior. Because of these differences, it is very important to know what *your* choice is. After all, if you don't know what choice you want your dog to make, how will your dog know what to do?

> **Scenario 1:** You are expecting company. The people that are coming over are your friends. They have met your dog in the past. Your friends and your dogs are friendly toward each other. You are in a room nowhere close to the door, and you have left the door unlocked in expectation of your friends being there at 3:00 p.m. Your dog is loose in the house, just hanging out. Your friends arrive early and unexpected at 2:45 p.m., knock on the door loudly, and come walking through the door, leaving the door wide open and yelling your name.
>
> *How do you want your dog to greet your friends that just burst into your house?*

Here are some of the common answers I get when I ask clients to answer the question above: "I don't want my dog to jump up on my friends," "I don't want my dog to run outside," "I am okay with my dog barking if people just came into my house, but I want my dog to be quiet when she knows they are not a threat," and "I want my dog to sit." Sound familiar?

When I ask this question, 99% of the owners tell me everything they *don't* want. Here is the problem; if you are only focusing on what you *don't* want, your dog will keep doing that thing. What happens in the moment of the greeting your friends is very reactive. You are actually waiting on your dog to do all of these behaviors you *don't* want instead of teaching your dog what you *do* want.

This is where it is important to really know what you want from your dog. In our podcasts and in my training sessions I call it, "Speaking in the Affirmative!" It is not enough to know what you want; it is important that you can put it into words. Once you put it into words, then you have the opportunity to actually see a behavior you want and praise for it. Knowing what you don't want is what you will correct for. Only knowing, speaking, and looking for what you don't want creates a situation in which that you only give attention to that behavior.

If you only correct for the behavior you don't want, and you never give attention when your dog makes a good choice, you create attention for that behavior. Your dog will keep doing that behavior for the attention. Remember the definition for praise: attention for any behavior when your dog makes a choice. I didn't say positive attention—I said attention. This means that if you only give attention to a behavior when it happens, and it is a behavior you don't want, even if you think you are correcting for that behavior, it is still attention. I use the example of the child that keeps getting in trouble for attention. Even though the attention is negative, that child keeps doing bad things because he gets attention for doing it.

Postulate: To understand what you want is most important. When you put behavior into terms of what you *don't want*, that behavior is the only thing that gets attention. Attention for a behavior reinforces that behavior, whether it is good or bad attention.

SPEAKING IN THE AFFIRMATIVE

How do you know when you are speaking in the affirmative or speaking in the negative? This is the practice of awareness I will be teaching about throughout the rest of this book. I stress awareness as an important key to understanding all of the tools for training and as the key to consistency. As I taught more people to train their dogs, I was exposed to more scenarios to look for the affirmative.

Using two of the most common behaviors people call me for help with, I created two scenarios to help you become aware of how you respond to your dog's actions. The scenarios will help you understand how you miss or don't look for the positive choices your dog is making. The reason I do this is to show you how your dog responds to attention, no matter what type of attention it is.

The first, and main, scenario I give is the one I mentioned above, which we will break down later. The second scenario I give is simple:

> **Scenario 2:** You go for a walk with your dog. While walking, on-leash, you encounter other dogs, people, and children. You don't have time to socialize, you just need to get your dog walked then get home.
>
> *How do you want your dog to behave on the walk with all of these distractions?*

41

Did you answer, "I don't want my dog to pull me on the leash?" That's the main answer I get. I also get, "I want my dog to walk without lunging after the other dogs," and "No barking!"

Because you have already gone through the first scenario above, you may have been thinking about what you really want. Here are other versions of the same answer. "Walk without pulling," and "Don't pay attention to the other dogs or people." Other times, I even get answers that are worded in the affirmative like, "I want my dog to walk on my right side." Or an owner may say, "I want my dog to stay with me in a heel."

All of those answers are very common. The main answers I get are the ones answered with negative words like "no," "without," and "don't." The tricky ones are the ones that sounded like they were answered in the affirmative. When using negative words, it is easy to turn around your thought or wording to work in the positive. "I don't want my dog to pull me." becomes, "I want my to dog walk with me, loose on the leash."

The answers that were stated in the affirmative are trickier because you then have to assess if the stated behavior is what you *really* want. Does your dog have to always be on your right side, for example? You do not have to be specific when describing what you want from your dog. Answering in general, affirmative language is best. "I want my dog to stay at my side," is much more general than saying I want my dog to stay at my 'right' side. Either works and one takes a lot less effort on your part.

Or, even better, the answer can be as simple as:

I want my dog to walk with me, loose on the leash.

This is an easy scenario, and with such a simple answer, stating things in the affirmative starts to become clear. Now what you are looking for when you take your dog for a walk is for her to walk with you, loose on the leash, and now you can praise her for the times she does just that. The biggest problem comes when you don't. When she is walking the way you want, loose on the leash, the normal reaction is to just walk. This is where awareness becomes very important.

I had a client once tell me he was not going to praise his dog for doing something it should be doing anyway. He was only going to praise his dog when it did something exceptional. When his dog made a decision to go over-and-above in the line of dog duty, that was when he deemed it worthy of praise. This is the attitude most people take, and this is a common mistake because you are reacting as if your dog has analytical thought.

> **Postulate:** Dogs are reactive. Good choices or bad choices become reinforced for the attention you give in the moment of the choice (or reaction) from your dog. Dogs do not analyze. Because of this, your dog does not make choices based on situational analysis.

The above client wanted his dog to make better decisions and to think about how to improve on the behavior, yet was never willing to teach his dog there were other decisions to make. Even in the case where a child continues to make bad decisions just to get attention, it is because good decisions were not rewarded, they were expected. Children can, and will analyze. They know that a better decision can be made and then they choose whether or not to behave that way.

Dogs do not think this way. Dogs are only reactive, so they will only react to what has gotten them attention in the past. With this mentality (and I think this is the mentality of most people, too; I know it was mine before I started to understand dog behavior), you will always get the bad behavior because you will only be reacting (giving attention) to the bad behaviors.

If you want your dog to go "over-and-above," you have to teach your dog what that looks like. You have to be aware that your dog is making the good choices and consistently praise those good choices in order to teach her what expectations you have. In the walking scenario, this means you have to consistently praise your dog when she is loose on the leash. Not only do you have to praise your dog for walking with you loose on the leash, you have to be aware of how many times you corrected your dog for any other behavior, such as lunging or pulling, and praise her ten times more than you corrected her for doing those behaviors you did not want.

By using that simple example of knowing what you want when your dog is walking on-leash, I hope you see the importance of being aware when your dog is behaving how you want and praising her in those moments.

Now that you are aware of how to respond from the above scenario, let's look back at the more complicated situation in Scenario 1. It is not as easy because it involves so many different behaviors and expectations from you. Let's look at how you would state all of those situations in the affirmative.

When friends or family enter my house, I want my dog to approach them in a way they are comfortable. A client said this to me once, and I thought it sounded wonderful, except it raises a question: What does that look like?

For me, it looks like this: I want my dog to stay on all four legs when greeting my friends. I want my dog to stay inside if the door is wide open. I want my dog to give space for people to come into my house. If my dog barks (which I am okay with, because people just came into my house), I want her to be quiet when I tell her. If my friends are giving my dog attention, it is okay if she hangs around them; if not, she needs to move on.

Every part of that scenario is answered affirmatively. It took me a long time to be able to word it all with favorable phrasing. It is not normal. What is normal is to react to all the behaviors we don't want. It is normal to expect your dog to do better each time this new scenario happens. When you correct your dog for bad behavior, you expect her to learn from this correction and change how she behaves. Herein lies the problem. You expect your dog to make a choice that you did not teach.

Until you can state your situation in the affirmative, you will only be reacting to that negative choice. You will become more corrective (or motivating) during that choice, and one of two things will start to happen. If you are too corrective, your dog will start to get fearful when people arrive and may even become protective or aggressive. If you are too motivational, your dog will expect you to act a certain way in order to behave in a certain way.

When you can state the behaviors you want in the affirmative, you are looking for and expecting very specific behaviors. Now, you can praise those behaviors. When your dog stays on all four legs, whether sitting or standing, while greeting your friends, you will be praising her. When your dog looks to go outside then chooses to stay inside, you will praise her. When your dog stops barking when you tell her, you will praise her. When your dog gives space, backs up, and allows your friends into your home, you will praise her. When your dog walks away from you and your friends, you will be aware she is making that choice and praise her.

This is when you are teaching your dog to make the choices you want. This is when your dog is starting to learn there are other choices to make. You have to stay consistent and continue to be aware that your dog is making these good choices.

> **Postulate:** Anything you do once or twice does not create a behavior or correct a behavior. The quicker you catch yourself and correct yourself, the quicker you and your dog will learn.

TOUCH

> **Postulate:** Touch is the biggest reward you can give your dog. Any time you touch your dog, you are rewarding whatever behavior your dog is doing at that time.

Any time you touch your dog, you are rewarding whatever behavior your dog happens to be doing at that time. I emphasize this statement over and over to an owner when I am training. This is a hard reality that most trainers do not teach. As a matter of fact, most trainers teach ways of correction through touch. I have seen this on TV, I have watched other trainers do some form of touch as a correction, and I have even known veterinarians that tell their clients ways to correct by touching the dog. As a trainer, it can be done in such a way to get the dog to stop doing what she is doing and pay attention. As an owner (or I say to owners, as a layman), it should not be taught. This is my personal opinion, and one I feel very strongly about.

Let's put this into context. If you have a small dog and you catch your dog pottying in the house, how do you get her to stop and go outside? If your small dog starts to run outside when the door is opened, how do you stop your dog from going outside? Most people say they would pick their dog up. If you have a medium or large dog (not so easy to pick up) and your dog is jumping up on your friends, how would you get your dog to stop jumping? If your dog is freaking out because of fireworks, how would you calm your dog down? Most people tell me they push them down to get them to stop jumping. Or, they say they will grab their dog during those sudden loud moments and try to calm the dog down by stroking or petting the dog.

All of these situations are ways that are inappropriate uses of touch. In each of the above situations, most people have to touch their dog in order to get them to stop the behavior. In each of those situations, you are reinforcing whatever your dog is doing by using touch. Without even realizing it, most people will reinforce the behaviors; pottying in the house, running outside, jumping up, and being scared of loud noises. Are you reinforcing or correcting the behavior you don't want?

Praise involves knowing that your dog made a choice, knowing that the choice was one you want your dog to make, then giving her positive attention at the time of that choice. This is when you are truly teaching your dog to be obedient.

MOTIVATE

Motivation is anything that you use to get your dog's attention and to make the choice you want her to make. Any time you can motivate your dog, she is more likely to remember what you want *and* want to do that thing. Motivation is a great tool; it is just not a great method of training because it creates expectation. In other words, if your dog expects something from you rather than doing it willingly, is she being obedient?

> **Postulate:** Motivation is anything positive you use to create a situation where your dog pays attention to you, then makes a choice. Anything overused as a motivation creates an expectation from your dog.

Motivation training is the most common method of training used today. What is the biggest form of motivation for most dogs? Treats or food. If you are using treats, or have used them in the past, you have seen how quickly your dog responds or reacts to them. If you continue to use that treat (or whatever form of motivation you are using), you will learn that sooner or later your dog will not perform the command unless you have the treat, pretend like you have the treat, or use some other form of motivation. You have now created an expectation from your dog. Your dog is more than likely only going to do something for you with reward or treat. You have to perform first because you have created an expectation from your dog.

I sometimes use this example: If I ask my daughter to take out the trash and she turns to me and says, "Yeah, give me my five bucks and I will," then I have overused money as a motivation. She now expects something from me (or I have to perform the act of reaching in my pocket and pulling out five dollars) in order for her to do what I asked. That doesn't really sound obedient, does it?

There is another big motivation frequently overused. What is it you normally say to get your dog's attention? That's right, her name. You think your dog will not do for you unless she is looking at you. Since that is the case, you use her name to get her to look at you. Or, you think that if your dog is not looking at you, she is not paying attention to you. Remember, motivation is *anything* you use to get your dog to pay attention and make a choice.

MOTIVATION AS A METHOD OF TRAINING

Have you ever noticed that sometimes, no matter how loudly or how many times you call, your dog still won't look at you? This is because you have overused her name as a motivation. She has learned that if she doesn't look at you, she won't have to do what you want. It is also because you are inconsistent with your expectations of your dog once she does look at you. Sometimes your expectation is positive. You want her to come in to eat. Sometimes your expectation is negative. You just found your favorite ball cap destroyed. Most of the time, your expectation is neutral. You just need her to come inside or go outside. Because of all of these and many more inconsistent scenarios, your dog has no real desire, or "want," to pay attention to you.

This is a big reason why motivation is a great *tool*, and not a good *method* of training.

In my podcast, Discover Your Dog: episode number 032, I discuss the differences between praise and motivation. I discuss the confusions that arise when you do not know the difference between each of these tools. When you overuse praise, it becomes motivation. It is no longer praise. This is a big reason why people confuse the two. Using treats, toys, body language, voice tone, or any other way to get your dog's attention, is using motivation in an appropriate way. When your dog makes a choice and you use any of those tools, it is praise.

When you look at it this way, a positive action can be motivation and motivation can never be praise. You can motivate your dog to make good choices by using things as toys, treats, body language, and voice tones. But, Praise is only when your dog makes the choice and you give attention to that choice.

It sounds so easy when put into the above terms, yet because of how you respond to many different behaviors in many different ways, it is important to be aware of the choices and reactions your dog is making at any given time. That is the trick; not that you react differently in different given times, but that you notice what you did and adjust your reaction the next time your dog responds in a certain way.

When you can recognize the difference between praising and motivating, then you can start making the adjustments in your training necessary to get the best reactions from your dog. As Devin, my co-host in the Discover Your Dog Podcast, puts it in every show, you will "demystify your dog's behavior so you can get the best out of your training."

CORRECT

A correction is anything that you do to get your dog to stop doing what she is doing and pay attention to you. Sometime this can be a quick pull to the leash and a verbal, "No." Sometimes it could just be the verbal "No."

> **Postulate:** Correction is anything negative you use to make your dog stop doing what she is doing and pay attention to you. Anything overused as a correction creates fear in your dog.

In training, I teach that "No" means "Stop doing what you are doing and pay attention to me." That's it, nothing else. Stop doing what you are doing and pay attention to me. If your dog is not doing what you want, correct. This means it is also important to know what you don't want because that is what you correct for. Herein lies the problem with most people. You think that if you can make your dog stop doing what she is doing, then *she will know* what decision to make.

This is also why most people overuse correction as a method of training. The goal, as I was taught when I first started learning how to train dogs, is to get the dog to stop a behavior by any means possible. Once the dog stops, then they *have* to make another choice. The only problem with this philosophy is how do you know the other choice is going to be the choice you want your dog to make if you don't teach her what that choice should be?

The way I train, and the way I was trained, is to do everything on the leash. The leash is used to get your dog to stop doing what she is doing and pay attention. There are two reasons for this.

One, so that you are not touching your dog. Remember, the biggest praise you can give your dog is touch. With the leash, you can physically make your dog stop doing what she is doing and pay attention.

The second reason is so that you have physical control. With the leash, you have the ability to make your dog do the things you want to teach her. Now you are getting down to the basic means of teaching your dog. You have the ability to get your dog to understand there is a choice. You get to create the choices you want by physically putting your dog into a given situation.

Because the leash is a tool used get your dog to make a choice, it is important to know when and what you are communicating at any given moment. I want to discuss importance of how to use your leash for the best possible outcomes when training your dog *not* to do something.

PROPER USE OF THE LEASH IN TRAINING

Any time you are going to correct, you must say "No" and pull on the leash. Any time you are going to pull on the leash, you must use the verbal command, "No." This is not about being inhumane, it is about getting your dog to *stop doing what she is doing and pay attention*. The whole, sole purpose of the leash is to get your dog to stop doing what she is doing and pay attention without touching her. Remember, the biggest praise you can give your dog is touch. This means if you have no way of making her stop a behavior other than touching her, you will be sending a very mixed message to her.

> **The Rule of No:** Whenever you say "No," you must pull the leash. Whenever you pull the leash, you must say "No."

Just as an example: You might catch your dog going to the bathroom in your house at an early age, when she is very small. When you catch her, you yell, swipe her up in your hands, then run her outside. Now, once outside, you continue to berate her for pottying in the house with an angry tone.

Here is what you communicated:

> When you yelled, she stopped: Correction. When you picked her up: Touch = Praise. Once outside, you set her down angrily and continue to yell at her so she will not finish: Correction? No; attention for the behavior of *not* going to the bathroom outside.

The correction stopped her from what she was doing and was appropriate. The pickup created unnecessary touching and is considered praise. This is a huge mixed message to your dog. Then you continue to be angry at your dog outside, and she now does not want to finish up out of fear. This could very well be a choice, or reaction, she is making at the time, out of fear, and now you are giving her attention for that choice. Any attention when your dog is making a choice is praise.

In the above example, if you had the leash on your dog, you could have grabbed the leash without touching her and corrected her that way. Then, as you got outside you could change your attitude, voice tone, and body language to put off positive, pleasing energy. Hopefully, your dog will finish pottying outside. You have now made outside a positive event and inside the negative event. By making outside a positive event, your dog will be more willing to go outside, and this will give you more opportunities to praise for the choice of going outside and teach her that is what you want.

THE RULE OF NO

I want to expand on this rule. If you are constantly saying "no" to your dog and never pulling the leash to make your dog stop doing what she is doing, your dog will soon learn that she does not have to do what you say. You may see her do things such as turn away, purposely not look at you, or just continue doing the behavior until you physically do something to stop her. She will soon learn that the word "no" means nothing. Again, because dogs are reactive, if you react to behaviors she is doing at the time (ignoring you), she will continue to ignore you because this is how you taught her to behave.

The other side of that rule is if you are constantly pulling on the leash without saying "no," your dog will soon learn she does not have to mind you *unless* she is on-leash. Have you ever noticed that your dog will behave better when she is on the leash rather than off the leash? This is because you are constantly using the leash to control your dog's actions without giving your dog the choice to make decisions and react appropriately. Shifting to a well-behaved and well-trained off-leash dog takes consistency and being aware of how you are teaching. If everything is about physical control, then that is what your dog expects when she is on-leash.

Near the end of this book, we will discuss the rules for training off-leash. Right now, you are practicing your awareness and consistency by keeping your dog on the leash and helping her learn to make choices.

To sum up the rule, the purpose of the rule is to get your dog to understand what the word "no" means even when she is off-leash. By pulling on the leash and saying "no" at the same time, you are making her stop doing what she is doing and pay attention. You are also putting a word with that physical action. By consistent association, you will create the expectation that when you say "no" years later, your dog will stop doing what she is doing and pay attention. What you do early in your dog's life to create good behaviors and great choices (or reactions) translates into a lifetime of good communication.

CORRECTION AS A METHOD OF TRAINING

Again, just as with motivation, correction is a good *tool*. It is just not a great *method* of training. If you overuse correction, you create fear. If your dog is doing something out of fear, or if she is not doing something out of fear, is she really being obedient? No.

One of the things I talk about in my sessions is the fact that dogs, like humans, are willing to test the boundaries of fear. As humans, we see stories all the time about how someone has either overcome fear to help another person or how people are going way beyond the limits of what we would consider a scary situation. I saw a man jump off a cliff with what looked like only his normal clothes on! As he spread his arms, there were small pieces of cloth attached to his arms and body like bat wings. He flew! That is way beyond my boundary of fear, but obviously not that guy's.

Dogs are not much different. Not because they make the conscious decision to test the boundaries, but because it is just in their nature, just as it is in ours. If you overuse correction, instead of creating a "want" in the dog to behave correctly, eventually your dog will take an opportunity to test the boundaries.

This example demonstrates what I mean. You may have heard of the electric fences people put around their yards that are buried underground. The dog wears a special collar when she is in the yard. If she gets too close to the underground wire, it beeps a warning, and then shocks the dog if she continues to get closer. When I ask the question, "Why does the dog not go near the boundary?" Most people answer because the dog will get shocked. This is not true. The dog does not go to the boundary because she is *afraid* of getting shocked. Notice the difference?

Some dogs do not fear this shock and can never be contained by these types of fences. I have seen dogs that run right through them, knowing the shock will last only a little while until they're on the other side. Yet, they will not go past the boundary to get back into the yard. They're willing to test it to get out, but not back in.

Once, I had a client that called and said that they were upset with the fencing person I recommended. The dog was continually getting out of the yard, and he thought the equipment was faulty. I called the fencing guy, and we agreed to all meet to see if we could rectify the situation. When we got there, I found out that the owner had run through four sets of batteries within a week. Bart, the fencing guy, checked all of the boundaries and equipment, and it was working just as it should.

He replaced the dead batteries in the collar then put the collar on the dog, and put her outside. After about 10 minutes, the dog went to the edge of the boundary and lay down. If you are familiar with the shock collars, some will beep a warning when the dog is close to the fence, prior to delivering the shock. This dog had tested that boundary enough to realize that when the beep stopped, there would be no shock. By lying in the beep zone, she would wear out the batteries. She did not realize she was killing the batteries; she just understood that no beep equaled no shock. Beep = Shock!

Bart recognized what this dog was doing and started laughing while explaining what was going on with this owner's dog. This is a prime example of how dogs are willing to test the boundaries. How did the owner get the dog to stay in the yard? He turned off the beep. The dog never heard the beep again, yet she would still get a shock when she got too close to the boundary. She may have tested it two or three times, got a shock, and after that was not willing to test it anymore.

One example I use to show how we, as humans, test the boundaries is if you approach your stove at home and see that glowing red spiral (or however your burner glows red), would you touch it? Why? Most clients answer "no," saying, "Because it is hot!" Then I reply by saying, "No, it is because you are *afraid* of being burned and each of us, at our own level, has a fear of being burned." To continue this scenario, let's just say you are in one of those large appliance warehouses looking for a new stove. You see the stove of your dreams on display in the center of the floor. Clearly, it is not plugged in, there is no gas connected, and yet there is a bright red display light right where a burner should be. It is an obvious fake and for display only. Would you touch it? I get all types of answers from this question. Everything from the few that say, "Not on your life," to the most common answer, "Heck yeah, I would." Because we all have a boundary of fear we are willing to go through; some would never test that boundary, yet many will. At some point and in some way in your life, you *all* will test, and have tested, the boundary of your fears.

How do I know this this is true? Because if you are reading this book, you crossed some line that said you needed help. You can't do it on your own. Sometimes, to me, asking or going to an outside source for an answer can be a big fear in itself. This also proves that once you have done something with consistency and it has worked, you are willing to do it again and again.

Fear is a good tool, if used appropriately. It is *not* a good method of training, and I can attest to this through experience. I was taught to train using the fear method of training. The people I worked with said, on more than one occasion, we were to break the dog down in order to build her up again. It makes the dogs miserable and their owners miserable. So, instead, I focus on Praise, with Motivation and Correction as tools to reinforce the message and help me train.

By now, you should be realizing that training your dog is not about your dog, it is about you. As in the scenarios discussed earlier, you see that adding practice times is necessary because of what you did and how you reacted. You have to be very aware of when and what choices your dog makes, and you have to behave appropriately during those times. As you learn more about how to get your dog to behave the way you want her to behave, you will see how this statement is very important in the process of learning how to communicate with your dog.

It does not end here. As I said earlier, you have to be very diligent with the homework. If you do put your dog into the behavior scene 19 more times over the next few days, do you think she will have to be corrected again? The answer is yes. As you do your part and increase the distractions and change the scenery, you will see your dog continue to test the boundary because she has not had enough praise situations in each scene you provide for her. Then, for every one correction you make, you have to add at least 10 more practice scenarios to your homework. This is why it takes so long and why so many people give up on their dogs. Or worse, why so many people give up on the behavior and then the dog does not get to participate fully with the family.

It took me a long time to really understand the true implications of this rule. First, it takes time. Think about it. How many times did you ever correct your dog for the behavior that finally frustrated you enough to buy this book? For every one of those corrections, you now need to get your dog into similar situations and praise her 10 times that number. This could be thousands or tens of thousands of times. It takes time!

In my scenario, after a lifetime of watching my Molly make the choice to stay on the floor, and being aware of her making the choice I wanted her to make, there was a certain point I had achieved. When I hit the ratio of praising my Molly 10 times more than I ever corrected her, she started making that choice on her own. You know how I know? She never got on the furniture, even when I wasn't home. She has no desire because she wants to stay on the floor. When I leave for long periods during the day, she is always on the floor. I know this because she sheds, and when she walks by my furniture it attracts her hair. She will go to people that are on the couch and want their attention, yet she stays on the floor and just gets close to them. Even when I visit friends and bring her with me, she chooses to stay on the floor at their home. It got to the point that testing her was no longer necessary. She had no desire to get on furniture. And still, when she made the choice with my friends (some of whom would have loved for her to get on the couch with them), I still recognized the choice and praised her for staying put, on the floor.

Now, I know there are people in this world that love to have their dogs on the furniture with them. I think this is awesome. This story has nothing to do with whether or not being on the furniture is bad, it is about understanding what you want and then praising your dog when she makes that choice. The choice here was for Molly to choose to stay on the floor in any given situation. Notice how I worded that. The choice was for Molly to choose to "stay on the floor," not for Molly to "stay off the couch" or "not get on the furniture." When you can put the behavior into terms of what you want, rather than what you don't want, you can see that there is a choice to be made and what the choice is. Putting it into terms of what you *don't* want only gives you one option. That option then is what gets attention and why your dog keeps doing that behavior. This is a tough concept to grasp.

CHAPTER 2

DEMYSTIFYING BEHAVIOR

Now that you have learned the basic tools for training and the methods to teach and train your dog, it is time to put them into practice. From this point on, you will learn how to make the three tools to work for you. You'll use them to learn how to communicate with your dog and make your dog a great part of your family.

We will also break down 23 more postulates and 13 more rules for training I have developed over the years. Many of these overlap, but have just enough of a difference that they each need to be discussed in detail. The difference between my rules and my postulates is that the rules are what I teach and tell my clients they have to do while training with me, while the postulates are just the way I believe things work.

There is an appendix at the end of this book that lists all of the rules and postulates in a neat, easy-to-access list. I have even created an extended form of each of the postulates that gives a brief (and sometimes not-so-brief) explanation of each.

From this point on, I will be discussing how I reached these conclusions and why I believe these different theories to be true. Most of the answers come from practice and participation. I practice my trade every day. There is not a day that goes by in my life that I don't talk about dogs, training dogs, dog behavior, or some other aspect of the dog training business. I "practice dog" in some way every day.

CONSISTENCY IS THE KEY

> **Postulate:** Consistency is the key to training your dog. You must know how you want your dog to behave, then act consistently in every given situation.

Yes, you all know what it means to be consistent. The problems come when you don't realize you are not being consistent. This takes awareness, and awareness comes through practice. Once you are aware of how you are communicating, then you can change it. If you are not aware, you cannot change.

Through practicing and teaching this awareness, I have learned that you may not realize you have done something until someone points it out. Once pointed out, you may do that one thing again 100 times before you ever learn to catch yourself doing it.

I like to use biting your nails as an example. I used to do this, and I know many people that still do. I remember many times where I only became aware I was biting my nails because someone would reach up and pull my hand out of my mouth. It took a very conscious effort to become aware that I was doing it and to eventually stop the behavior.

Similarly, many owners don't notice the things they do with their dogs. Often, I ask an owner to tell their dog to sit. The owner, who has told me their dog knows this command, will say the command to the dog, and the dog will not react. Before the owner even realizes it, usually after I have pointed it out, they have repeated the command many times. If I ask them later to tell me how many times they said the command before the dog sat, they are rarely able to answer correctly because they were not aware. The habit of repeating the command multiple times has become so ingrained that when it happens, it seems natural.

Sometimes, I have to point it out many times over the course of months for the awareness to set in. Even then, when I am no longer doing the training, old habits will creep back in and the repetitions begin. This is why it is so difficult to be consistent; you are only vaguely aware of when you are not being consistent. If you have no awareness at all, the habit will never change.

Is it wrong to repeat a command? No, but the point of any method or tool of training is that you have to know what you are communicating in every given situation. You should say a command only once and always expect your dog to do that command. Once you repeat the command, it is no longer a command. It now becomes motivation.

From our rules, you know that anything overused as a motivation creates an expectation. When you repeat a command, typically you will raise your voice or follow the repetition with body language. Once you do either of these things, your dog will begin to expect you to do these things every time. Your dog will wait until you reach a certain tone with the command or use certain body language prior to doing that command. Your goal should always be to say something once, then expect your dog to react. Anything you do after that one time becomes a way to get your dog's attention, and if you continue that action, your dog expects that action every time. Repeating the command, moving your body so your dog will see you, raising your voice, or even saying your dog's name are all motivation techniques that you don't even realize you are doing.

Being aware of this is very difficult. If you start to become aware when you are repeating the command, you then have to change how you respond to your dog. This is where the practice comes in. If you are not practicing how you communicate to your dog with intention, you will never be able to break the habit of miscommunication. With practice, you start to recognize your inconsistencies more often. The more you practice, the quicker you realize what you're doing and the more consistent you become.

LEARNING WHAT YOU ARE COMMUNICATING

This brings me to a big point I always try to make: It is not the style or method of training you use that is important. What is important is that you know *what* you are communicating in every given situation. The same end result in training or behavior can be reached in many different ways. Every trainer uses the same tools; it is the tool used in any given situation that determines the method of training for that behavior. This is also why there are so many differing thoughts on how to handle different situations.

My goal is to teach you what you are communicating in every situation. Once you know what you are communicating, you can decide how to proceed and how you want to continue the process. You get to make the choice. In the Discover Your Dog Podcast Episode 032, Praise vs. Motivation, I talk about gaining friends by giving out $100 bills. Some may consider this a crazy way of gaining friends and others may think it is a great idea. Neither person is wrong. It is just a matter of opinion and perspective.

This is why I stress that you must understand what you want in any given situation. When you have the correct goals in mind and understand what you are communicating, then you are on the right track to getting your dog to willingly behave the way you expect. That is the key. You want your dog to do what you expect, willingly, or as most understand when it comes to dogs, obediently.

WHAT CREATES CONSISTENCY?

When I ask this question, my thought is that consistency is a habit. I have to do something over and over to create a habit. Once I create that habit, I don't have to even think about it. The unfortunate part of that type of thinking is that for the extreme circumstances you face in your life, even if you have developed good habits, you may react very differently.

Consistency is created through confidence. Just because you have not created a habit, it does not mean that you can't act consistently. It comes down to catching yourself when responding to a choice or reaction from your dog, knowing what you communicated when you responded to that choice, and then changing your actions accordingly. This allows room for error. It also requires that you learn what you are communicating in every situation and evaluate that action. Is that action what you meant, and is it teaching your dog to behave in a way you expect? If so, continue that action. If not, change. Anything you do once or twice does not create a behavior. The consistency and repetition, using the 10 to 1 rule, will create the behavior you desire.

Actions create results, which create your point of view. This is why so many people see things differently when it comes to training your dog. If a trainer sees the results of treat training and concludes, in their mind, that it works, this then becomes their *point of view*. You may agree or disagree with the point of view of a treat trainer. If a trainer sees results in correcting a behavior from a dog and then continues to use correction as a method to get a dog to quit certain behaviors, correction becomes that trainer's *method* of training any behavior. Again, you may agree or disagree with this method. This is why there are so many different ways of handling any one behavior.

Any method you choose to train your dog comes from what you have seen and heard work. This is also why so many differing styles of training work and are proven to work every day. I have learned from using all of these tools that motivation and/or correction tools, used as methods of training, will not work on every dog. Only praise, used appropriately and understood for what it is, works on every dog in every given situation. Teaching you this method is what this book is about.

In addition to consistency, you must understand how your energy affects your dog training and how the hierarchy affects how dogs learn. These three things are basics needed to achieve your goals, you will need to understand why and how your dog is behaving and reacting certain ways to you, your family, and your social circles.

CONTROLLING YOUR ENERGY

Energy is what you exert when working, playing, or just hanging out with your dog. This energy is reflected by your dog. Think of your leash as a conductor of whatever you are feeling at the time.

The energy you are communicating to your dog is comprised of the emotions you are feeling at the time. Your dog will mimic this energy, depending on the situation and level of connection you have with your dog. The point in training is to create a bond and improve communication. Stronger bonds and better communication create a higher level of connection with your dog. As this connection gets better, your dog will better reflect the energy you have.

> **Postulate:** The energy or emotions you emit when working, playing, or just hanging out with your dog will radiate to your dog. Your dog will mimic this energy depending on the situation and level of connection you have with your dog. Think of your

> leash as a conductor of whatever energy you are feeling at that time.

I like to call your leash a conductor because this is the line you have been using to create this connection. How you handle the leash lets your dog know how much you trust her. If you are constantly pulling, guiding, or tugging, then that level of trust is low. Your dog will know this. It becomes very frustrating for your dog, and that reflects back on you as well. This is why I tell you, the owner, to let your dog make the choice, then react to the choice appropriately.

For example, one of the biggest behavior problems I work on is how the dog greets someone at the door. First, you have to know the triggers. Then, you have to know if you are prepared appropriately for the greeting. What triggers your dog to get excited? A knock? The doorbell?

Once you know the trigger, you then have to be prepared to act (and react) the right way so you can teach your dog how to respond to the trigger. There are two scenarios here. In one, you knew the people were coming and in the other, you didn't know someone was going to be at the door.

Both situations offer many different ways for you to react to your dog, which can create many different behaviors. Did you hold her back? Did you yell at her while she continued to jump, bark, or do whatever it is you want to correct? Did the person at the door love and pet on her when they arrived?

All of the reaction questions above are normal actions, but they continue to reinforce the bad behavior. Holding your dog back is touching your dog. Yelling at her without her stopping the behavior and her not paying attention to you is attention for the behavior. If the person at the door gives attention, especially loving and praising attention, it is also a reinforcement of whatever behavior she is doing. Remember, it is up to you to recognize how you *want* your dog to behave, create *that* choice from your dog, and love on your dog when she has made the choice.

This is just one scene in a day full of actions, interactions, and reactions between you and your dog. Usually in this type of scenario, the energy is high. It could be fun and spirited energy, or it could be frustration and anger. Either way, there is tension and attention to the trigger of someone being at the door.

Let's say you were prepared for this person to visit. When the knock happens, your dog will react in the same way. Being prepared, you have your leash on your dog. When you go to the door to greet your friend, you hold back on the leash to keep your dog from jumping or running out the door.

How is your energy? Are you frustrated because this behavior continues to happen? If so, you will see that frustration come from your dog in the form of digging her paws into the floor to get to the person. Just as you are frustrated, she is very frustrated at being held back. At this point, you are not letting your dog make a choice at all. You are using the leash for what I call "Avoidance Training." You are avoiding the chance to let your dog know how you want her to behave, because you already know how your dog will behave. In this case, you will continue to see this behavior because you have never taught your dog how you want her to behave in this situation.

What do you want your dog to do when greeting your friend? Stay on all four legs. Now that you have a behavior to look for, you can get your dog to make a choice. Using the leash, allow your dog to approach your friend. If she jumps, quickly say no, pull her about five to 10 feet away from the person of interest, and get her to focus on you. Once focused, re-approach your friend. Now you are creating a space for learning, and your energy is focused on looking for appropriate behaviors instead of reacting to inappropriate behaviors. In situations like this, I find I am much more patient and calm when I work with a purpose. If this is how you are feeling, your dog will soon pick up on that energy and act accordingly.

In most cases you do expect guests and can be prepared. If you have an unexpected guest, this creates a different set of problems. You still must be aware of how you expect your dog to behave in the moment of greeting that guest and if you don't have a leash on your dog you also have to realize you are going to inadvertently reinforce any bad behaviors. For example, if your dog stays on all fours when greeting, it is up to you to recognize this and praise your dog in that moment. If she jumps up the only way you are going to stop your dog is to grab (which is touching) and hold your dog back. At that moment, you need to get the leash so that you can better correct (and praise when your dog makes the right choice) for the jumping up. You also have to realize you have created more work for yourself because of the attention you gave your dog in that moment. It is not a bad thing, you now have to create it that your dog chooses to stay on all fours ten times for that one time you gave attention to the behavior.

Through this example, I have described how your energy can create a learning situation for your dog in each scenario. It is important that you recognize this in every situation, every day, with your dog. For the most part, your dog is just going to be hanging out with you throughout the day. She will be well-behaved, and you will be doing the things you normally do.

During those hangout times, you may notice different behaviors. These are times your dog may be cueing in on your feelings or energy. Have you ever noticed that when you feel really good and excited, your dog seems to be easily excitable? Even in those lazy hangout times, you may be sad or upset and your dog is just lying at your feet or is there to comfort you.

I believe dogs can show emotion. For the most part, their emotions are basic and driven out of fear or love, yet there have been some amazing stories of how dogs have faced down fears, supported whole families, and even died when an owner was no longer around. I believe these emotions are learned from and strengthened by the owner. The stronger the connection is with an owner, the more obvious the emotional reactions from a family/fused dog will be.

You have to learn to keep some of these emotions in check if you want to have a really good bond with your dog. For example, if you were to catch your dog going to the bathroom in the house and you get angry, that anger stays with you for a long time. If you are still angry when you finally get your dog outside, then outside becomes a negative place to potty as well. This is why many domesticated dogs hide to go to the bathroom. You may also stay mad and expect to find an accident every time you come home. Now your dog starts to have negative reactions to you coming home. Hiding, cowering, not greeting you at the door, and tearing items up while you are gone are all things that could be a reaction to you coming home angry. The problem will get worse and worse. You have the ability to correct the behaviors; you just have to adjust your energy.

You have to be aware of what energy you are transmitting to your dog. In many situations, it is not a big deal. Because dogs are very good at learning you, your body language, and your voice tones, your dog knows when you are serious or not and can adjust her energy accordingly. If you are having an issue with a behavior that does have an emotional tie to it, you must be very careful how you approach the training and what level of praise, motivation, and correction you use.

UNDERSTANDING THE HIERARCHY

HOW DOGS VS HUMANS VIEW THE HIERARCHY

Dogs live in a hierarchy. One of my clients, who was also a veterinarian, told me once, "It is unfortunate that there was not an Abraham Lincoln in the dog world to let them know that all dogs were created equal." When you go into a room full of people, you assume everyone in the room is of equal stature until you are told or find out otherwise. Even then, there are others in the room that you still consider equals, some that you consider below you, and some you consider above you in the hierarchy.

You can't help it; it is human nature and a survival instinct to create these rankings. You make assumptions because you can analyze. This analytical thought allows you to change your point of view based on the actions you see or do. In other words, if something was to change in your household, you are able to change your position and ranking in the hierarchy.

Dogs do not view the world this way. In a dog's eyes, her pack is ranked. If there are a total five people and dogs in a room, the dog views them as 1, 2, 3, 4, and 5. Let's say the five are three people and two dogs. Father, mother, child, Molly (the first dog to arrive in the family), and Oz (the second dog to arrive in the family).

A person would rank Dad and Mom equal (1 and 1), the child next (2), then the dogs. Because you had Molly first, you rank her 3, then because Oz came into the scene last, you rank him 4. This ranking is very common, but this causes many families to have behavior issues. Humans and adults rank each other as equals and the child below. This is a natural ranking in the human family. Molly is ranked 3rd, below the child, only because she has been part of the family longer and Oz is ranked last. Again, this is the human ranking, and because of it there is an immediate communication breakdown.

As stated above, the dogs see every member as their own rank. For example, Molly may view the pack as Father – 1, Oz – 2, Molly – 3, Mother – 4, and Child – 5. You are part of your dog's ranking, and you are part of your dog's pack. Where you are in the pack, and where your dog views herself in the ranking, determines her job and her behaviors. It is the dominant's job (I will refer to this member as the "leader") to keep order and peace in the pack. If there are squabbles amongst the other pack members, the leader will determine whether or not she should intervene. If you see situations in your family in which your dog tries to get in between two people, shows aggression when aggression is present, seems very aloof toward most of the members of the family (this is the most common behavior of a leader), or her actions or reactions only happen when there is a threat toward herself, then you are seeing signs that a dog has taken or will take a dominant role in your family.

> **Postulate:** Dominance is about trust. If your dog trusts you will be consistent, she is less likely to test the boundaries. When you create trust, you create great communication and an incredible bond between you and your dog.

In the dog world, the highest participant in the pack is the one that is the most consistent and trusted. Dogs look to other dogs and humans to be protectors and faithful pack members. Dogs are also much more consistent than humans. That is why consistency is so important in training. It is something that dogs need and understand.

The reason we have dogs as pets in the first place is because of the ability of a dog to accept the lower pack order. Problems arise when humans want them to be higher in the pack order (with or without knowing it) or when inconsistent human behaviors confuse the dog. This confusion, or lack of good communication, takes away the dog's trust and makes it so the dog must continue to test for a higher rank in the hierarchy.

This is why I tell many owners that dog is dog's best friend, not man's best friend. Why? Because dogs understand each other much better than they understand us. As dogs become more and more domesticated, I see that even the dogs' communications among each other are starting to grow further apart.

> **Postulate:** Dog is dog's best friend! Dogs understand each other much better than they understand humans.

It is important to know what the dog's hierarchical view of the world is. In a dog's mind, if you are not the leader and you are getting attention, it is the leader's job to get rid of the lower pack member. Your dog does not have the ability to reason with you. You are not going to be able to convince your dog that she is higher or lower than another member of the pack. Only that other member can make that determination.

Yes, I said the only member that can change the pack level is the one that is being challenged or tested. This means you (or your child, your spouse, or any other human) are not going to change the level in the hierarchy. What it does mean is that you should have such a high level of dominance (trust) from your dog that even in situations where she perceives another member to be lower than her, she will still make the choices you expect her to make.

You have to take the leadership role so your dog looks to you when making choices. You also have to let your dog know what you expect of her in all of those situations. You have to teach your dog how to behave around your children or spouse, and how to behave socially. If other members of your family also take a higher role with your dog, then your dog will start to relax more. The more consistent each family member is, the more your dog feels she can just be a dog.

This is one reason I like to work with whole families rather than just one or two members. Small children may not be able to do the training and may be viewed as lower in the hierarchy by your dog, yet you, the owner, can show your dog how to behave around your children. Your children can also be taught the proper way to handle themselves. In situations where a child is very young, I have seen them mimic the parent and create the same results with a dog as the adult did.

I am going to get a little extreme in the following example, but it will demonstrate the hierarchy and the way your dog views life in the pack. If you are viewed lower in the hierarchy in your dog's mind and someone that is viewed higher is giving you unsolicited attention, in order for your dog to get the attention she is supposed to get, she has to kill you. This is her way of removing the lower-level pack member and getting the attention she feels she deserves.

So, when you are seeing your dog growl at one of your children while you are giving them attention, this could be a pack reaction. If you move your dog when on the couch, and she gets aggressive toward you, this is a pack reaction. If your dog urinates on personal items of yours, or someone else's in the family, this is a pack reaction. A dog humping a human or another dog is also a pack reaction.

Your dog is not going to have a conversation with you and explain to you that you should be giving her attention instead of giving it to lower members in the pack. Your dog is not going to set a family meeting and let everyone vote to determine their place in your home. Your dog is not going to analyze the situation and decide that she should just accept a lower place in the hierarchy. No, your dog is going to react and respond the only way she knows how to survive. How you respond in that moment is either going to correct the situation or reinforce the situation.

When you understand a dog's reactive behavior, you will understand why you reinforce the behaviors you don't want. Your dog does not care whether or not you are her best friend. Your dog does not care that you yell at her when she is doing something wrong. Your dog does not understand that you are trying to correct her for behavior you don't want her to do. Your dog doesn't actually understand English.

What your dog understands is that she can or cannot act in a certain way in a certain situation. Not only that she can or cannot, but also that you allow her to behave that way in that situation. If you have an idea of what is going on in your dog's head, you have a better chance at responding correctly.

APPROPRIATE ACTIONS AND REACTIONS

It is important to learn to react to your dog's behavior in appropriate ways in order to get your dog to understand what you want from her or how you expect her to behave. Dog owners typically fall into the trap of only reacting to bad behaviors, and usually inappropriately. This inappropriate reaction creates mistrust from your dog, mainly because you react to the bad behaviors differently every time. Once you may yell, once you may "knee" your dog, once you may push your dog down off of you, or once you may tell your dog to do a command (sit or down), then stroke or try to calm your dog. All of these are very different reactions from you for the same behavior of jumping up.

Another example of inconsistent human behavior is how you use commands in different situations; it is confusing for your dog. The best example is the "Come" command. "Come" should mean one specific thing. In the Discover Your Dog Podcast Episode 002, Specificity, we talk about the importance of understanding the purpose of the basic commands. "Come" is used in so many inconsistent ways that it is difficult for your dog to grasp this command. "Come" to come inside, "Come" to go outside, "Come" to go for a ride, "Come" to eat, "Come" to play . . . There are so many ways you use that word (even though you think you are giving a command) in so many situations that the word "come" becomes confusing to your dog.

Performing different actions in the same situations is very confusing for your dog. If your dog is seemingly being defiant or stubborn in situations you thought you were being consistent, the truth is that you aren't. This is why your dog behaves in a defiant or stubborn way.

The more consistent your actions are, the more your dog will trust that you are going to act in a certain way, and the more likely it is that you will take the dominant role. Your dog will stop testing the boundaries of the hierarchy. Most dogs want this structure. They want *you* to take the role as the dominant, and

75

they want to trust you. When you take this role, they get to be a dog. I say *most* because a very small percentage of dogs are truly dominant dogs. They do not make good pets.

CHAPTER 3

TRAINING PROGRESSION

GETTING STARTED

In this book, I will not be writing about how to train commands nor will I be teaching you how to stop certain behaviors you may be looking to correct. From here on, you will be learning how to get the best results from training and why certain things work and others don't.

The purpose of this book is to teach you how to communicate. Once you have learned what you are communicating in any given situation, then you will know how to get your dog to make the choices you want her to make. Figuring out those choices is up to you. I can only give suggestions and examples based on what I would want my dog to do and how I would expect my dog to behave. You are going to have differing ideas and opinions on what it means for your dog to be a great member of your family. I love that people have those differing ideas and opinions; they are what drove me to teach and train, and why I teach the way I do.

It is not my job to point out every problem with your dog. It is not my job to tell you how your dog should or should not behave in any given situation. Why is that not my job? Because I am only going to be in your life for a brief moment, and each of us has different expectations.

It is my job to teach you how, and what, you are communicating to your dog. Even now while you read this book, I am only in your life for a brief moment. What you do when you have finished this book is up to you. How you behave, how you choose to continue to communicate, and what you choose to take as important or not important is totally up to you. How much you choose to work with your dog, how many sessions a day, how many people you choose to expose your dog to, and how you choose to expose your dog to the world is up to you. The same goes for me. If I want a well-trained, well-behaved, and well-socialized dog, then it is up to me to put in the work.

The other reason it is not my job is because everybody has different expectations from their dog. Some people love when their dog jumps up on them, some don't. Some people allow their dogs on the furniture, some don't. It is not right or wrong; it is just personal preference. This is also why it can be difficult to correct a behavior if everyone in the household is not onboard with the training or expectations.

From this point forward, the rules and postulates I cover are about the work. The work, of course, is up to you. I work with people of all skill levels and all ages. They get dogs with varying degrees of intelligence and personality. I didn't match them up; they chose each other. Once I am in someone's home, it is my job to work with both the dog's and the human's personalities to teach them how to fuse together into one family and have the best experience possible.

Humans do have personalities that are very different from one person to the next. When working or communicating with your dog, you have to recognize this. When people do not know I am a dog behaviorist and they are talking about their own dog, they may have a very different opinion of how their dog should behave in social situations. I love to hear people give advice to others about how to handle a situation with their dog, not knowing that I do this for a living. There are so many opinions and schools of thought when it comes to handling certain situations. Those differing opinions come from both that individual's personality and their **method of training** when it comes to communicating with a dog. Choosing a method is different than choosing what tool to use at the time. Your method defines your style and belief when it comes to training your dog.

WHAT FIRST?

You have probably had your dog for a while. You have already established a relationship and some sort of communication. Because you already have this starter point, it is a little different than when I start working with a new client.

The first thing I do with a client is establish a relationship. Because I am going to be in a family's home for two to three months, it is important that I can work with them and they can work with me. I do this by sitting down with them for about 45 minutes before even meeting the dog. This time is important to establish what they already know and to tell them how we are going to accomplish their goals through training. For most families, the goals are not learning the commands, but instead involve stopping some behavior or establishing boundaries to prevent a behavior. This is why I say we are going to accomplish their goals *through* training.

This very important introduction is the same with the dog. When you greet your dog for the first time, you are establishing the boundaries, communicating how you want your dog to behave, and revealing your weaknesses to your dog. The better you can communicate in these early stages, the better your results will be.

During this initial "learning each other" period, you have to establish ground rules. This is just like when I go over the contract and talk about the training tools with a new client. This grace period is important for learning whether you and your dog's personalities clash or connect. I look at this relationship with you and your dog on that very first meeting as well.

For the most part, dogs and humans belong together and get along just fine. There are, just as in any relationship, minor things that need to be worked out. Occasionally, the personalities clash. This is not impossible to work on, it just takes a concentrated effort and willingness to work through these differences from the owner. It is hard work. Not because it is physically hard (although that can be the case sometimes), but because it is not our normal way of thinking. It takes awareness. The more stubborn, active, silly, that your dog is, the more stubborn, active, and willing to work through the silliness you have to be. The issue is not the compatibility; it's the willingness to work. Are you willing?

BEGINNING YOUR RELATIONSHIP

In the beginning, you have to set the boundaries. Setting these boundaries and creating structure will make your dog feel more comfortable around you. Dogs want boundaries and rules. Not every dog is going to just obey your wishes, so you must communicate what the rules are. Then, you have to stay consistent and abide by the rules as well.

I start this process by teaching an owner how to casually walk with their dog. The walk is one of the things you do most often. It can be frustrating or pleasing, but it's an important way to set the stage for future training.

Anything you want your dog to do will take time. It is not natural for a dog to be on a leash, nor is it natural for you to guide an animal around the neighborhood. The boundaries have to be established. When walking, you should be praising your dog when the leash is loose. The second it goes tight, you have to stop, change directions, or find some other way to make your dog go back to walking loose on the leash.

In this case, it is up to you to teach your dog what you want as well as what you don't want. You do this by changing directions or stopping every time the leash goes tight. When the leash goes tight you should say, "No", then change directions. You may also go silent, as in this case ignoring the tight leash is an appropriate correction as well. The temptation is to try to explain to your dog what you want, but if you start talking to your dog while the leash is tight, you are giving her attention for the behavior.

Similarly, if your dog goes tight on the leash and you pull her back to you but continue moving forward, your dog has not stopped doing what she is doing to pay attention to you. More than likely, she is going to move quickly to the end of the leash again.

When you are working on any behavior or command, you need to understand that it is going to take 30 to 45 days in a row of praising your dog for making the decisions you want. Even if you get only one praise that day, you still have to keep working. Even if you get a dozen praises by day 10, you have to keep working. You can measure this on a daily calendar if you are organized and diligent enough, or you can keep track by using the **Ten to One Rule** that we discussed. We go in-depth on the rule in the Discover Your Dog Podcasts Episodes 016 and 017 and the appendix of this book. By using the **Ten to One Rule**, you don't have to keep up with the number of days, only how many praise opportunities you owe your dog.

This is why you should be diligent with the practice; not to correct your dog, but to be aware of praise opportunities. The better your dog gets at walking loose on the leash, or any other behavior, the more distractions you should expose her to. This is not for her to work through the distractions, but for *you* to work through them and continue working on your awareness of your dog's behavior.

In this basic exercise of walking loose on-leash, you can now start looking for other situations in your life when your dog is making good decisions and praise for them as well.

After about a week of working on the loose leash, it is time to start on the basic commands. I go through each of the commands I teach in a specific order: Sit, Heel, Come, Down, and Place. The progression is important because each command builds on what you learned before.

If you are in a class or in some way learning how to do each of these commands, I suggest you go about one to two weeks working on any one command, then add the next command to your routine. Your dog does not have to master any one command before moving on; however, if she doesn't know the Down command, she can't do the Place command yet.

Before we get into each command individually, you need to know a few things. My intention is not to teach you how to do each command, although you may get that from each section. I am explaining the purpose for the each of the commands. I am also explaining why I proceed in the order I do. Lastly, I am talking about you. You, the dog lover, are the one that I am training, not your dog. Everything I write about from here on is about you, how you should behave, what you should be looking for, and how you should respond to many situations.

Unfortunately, I cannot cover every situation, but if you pay attention to who I am training, then you will learn how to work with your dog in any circumstance.

A BREAKDOWN OF THE BASIC COMMANDS

SIT

> **Postulate:** The Sit command is just getting your dog to sit. It is not about focus or correction, although the Sit command is used for these two reasons more often than any other command.

Sit is sit. That's it! When teaching this command, it is the first command I work on with an owner because it gives great opportunities for you to look for praise situations. When you give this command from the beginning, you want to work on a few things.

First, stay still. When you give the Sit command, stop or be still. Giving a Sit command while moving is a little more advanced, and you want to give your dog every reason to be successful.

Only say the command once. When you, the owner, repeat a command to your dog, it communicates two things: One, you did not mean it the first time and, two, your voice tone changes when you repeat the command. Two, it becomes motivation, as we discussed in detail in the section on motivation.

If you felt you had to say the command twice, it was because you did not have the confidence in yourself to know whether or not your dog knows the command. If you confidently knew your dog did not know the command, you would have just reached down and put her into the command. If you confidently knew your dog knows the command, you would have reacted with a correction.

Also, your voice changed. Your dog will quickly pick up on the change of tone and then only respond when she knows you are serious. You may have thought you were serious at first, but when you repeated the command, the next time you said it you were a little more serious, then a little more serious, and then very serious. By the time your voice reached this level, more than likely you were angry or frustrated. If your dog did happen to sit at this point, you are also more than likely not going to praise her.

> **Postulate:** Your voice tone is a main way your dog learns from you. A dog can pick up subtle changes in your voice and will respond according to your level of sincerity. Coupled with body language, these are the two most important communication tools you use when communicating with your dog.

A dog can pick up on subtle changes in your voice that you may not even realize you are making. There is a level you reach where your dog realizes the next action you make is going to result in something bad. This is when she reacts. I relate it to parents that count to three when they have told their children to do something. What did one and two mean? Nothing! Three is the magic number and what will make the child react.

Practice saying the Sit command when your dog is not looking at you. The real practice is that you just say the command and expect the behavior. Whether your dog is looking at you or not makes no difference. This is true with not just the Sit command, but every command you give. If you constantly make your dog look at you when you give a command, she will quickly learn that if she is not looking at you when you speak, she does not have to do what you said. I have even seen dogs look away from an owner right after the owner gives a command.

Say the command and only the command. I have a client that says "all right" before every command. It is so ingrained in his dogs that I also had to start saying "all right" before every command to get the dogs to listen. "All right-Sit" is now the command for him.

The same goes with your dog's name. Leave it out of the command unless you have multiple dogs and want only one particular dog to do what you are asking. You say your dog's name because you want her to look at you (or to get her attention). You do not need your dog to be looking at you to pay attention. The practice of saying the command and only the command is a practice in awareness. Most people never even realize they have said the dog's name or made any other sound.

Once you have given this command, the expectation is (or should be) that your dog holds that command until you release her. All commands should have a release command as well, so that your dog learns that a command is something she is doing for you. If you just say a command and your dog does that command but then does whatever she wants right after, you have not established enough boundaries. By getting up whenever she wants, your dog is taking control of the workout. If she can have this little bit of control during an obedience command, she will continue to test the boundaries in other areas of your life. I use the command, 'All-Done'. Some people say 'Free Dog' or 'Free.' Either works as long as you use the same phrase every time.

What is the purpose of Sit? Nothing. Sit is just Sit, as I said at the beginning of this chapter. Now, if I can get my dog to sit in a very distracting situation, I am teaching her to pay attention to me and be obedient. Sit will not fix a behavior or calm her down. Once you release her, she still has to make decisions based on the environment and distractions presented to her at that time.

It is like sitting your kid in a chair to have a talk. Sitting in the chair had nothing to do with the behavior; it was just a means to create focus. If anything, the Sit command can be used to create a little focus, but you still have to respond in an appropriate way when your dog is released.

The difference between making your kid sit to focus and making your dog sit to focus comes during the release. When you tell your kid to get up, they have the ability to analyze what you said and act according to the consequence they are willing to face from their actions. A dog is going to act at the moment of release, and how you react to your dog will let her know whether or not you want her to continue the behavior.

SUMMARY

- Stay still.
- Say the command only once.
- It is not necessary that your dog is looking at you.
- Say only the command. Don't use your dog's name or any other attention-getting sound.

HEEL

Heel means for your dog to walk at your left side and sit when you stop. The Heel command is the most misunderstood command of all of them. In my workouts, Heel is just that, the workout. I compare the Heel command to going to the gym. In the Discover Your Dog Podcast, Episode 033, we discuss how Heel is like the warm-up. It is the part of the training you do to get your dog focused and to let your dog know she is now in workout mode.

Heel is a formal command with the release command to be said at the end. When you say, 'Heel' your dog is to walk at your left side and sit when you stop. Most people say this word without knowing what they are asking and expecting the dog to instinctively know that this means to walk with you. Heel is only to be used in a formal workout. I also see people confuse the Heel command with the Come command. In more advanced training, Heel does serve other purposes, but in this book, it should be used only for the basic use of getting your dog prepared for a workout.

> **Postulate:** The Heel command is about focus for your dog. This is the command used to warm up, get ready to work, and start the workout. Heel is rarely used in everyday situations.

To practice this command, you have to make your dog stay at your left side. When she is too far out in front, or too far behind, she is not in a heel. Your dog's front legs, when standing still, should be even with your heel. Also, if you are standing still, your dog should be in the Sit position. Sit is part of the Heel command. When walking, your dog should be walking with you loose on the leash at your left side. Your dog cannot sniff around, or go pee on something, and still be in the Heel. This is a very formal and strict command. The better you are at keeping your dog in this command, the better your dog will also be on normal walks.

As I said before, Sit is incorporated in the Heel command. When you stop, your dog must sit. If you have given the Heel command, the Sit should be automatic. You should not have to tell your dog anything else. Also, you have to release your dog from the Sit. In order to release your dog from any command you have to use a release phrase or word that lets your dog know she is done with that command or give another command.

That brings me to the casual walk I wrote about at the beginning of this chapter. Heel is not for the casual walk. Again, your dog cannot pee, sniff, or greet other people or dogs when in the Heel command. When you are going for these casual walks, you should just stick with keeping your dog loose on the leash. In the casual walk, it is okay for your dog to be on either side, a little in front, or a little behind. To ask your dog to heel during a casual walk is a misuse of this command.

SUMMARY
- Note that the purpose in Heel is to get your dog ready to work out.
- Practice making your dog stay at your heel.
- Sit is part of the Heel command.
- Heeling your dog is unnecessary in casual walks.

COME

I feel this is the most misused and confusing of all the commands. Misuse of this command can be very confusing to the dog. The Come command means your dog comes to you and sits. As with the Heel command, your dog should stay in a Sit until you release her or give her another command.

When I teach this command to owners, I tell them it is about learning to be specific when communicating with the dog. Dogs have a very limited vocabulary. Even if a dog knew over 100 words, this is still a very small percentage of words compared to the human. It is a lot for a dog. Because of this, you need to pick your words and their meanings wisely.

The trouble with the word "Come" is that you use it in many different situations. "Come" to come inside, "Come" to go outside, "Come" to eat, "Come" to go for a walk, or "Come" to go for a ride. The Come command should only mean one thing: "Come to me and sit."

A dog will decipher your voice tones and eventually know what you mean with the different uses of "Come," yet that process can take a long time, and you are still being inconsistent. You can use other words for those other things, like "Come on," "Let's go," or "Let's walk." Your dog will have a better idea of what you want from those phrases.

Focus on being specific with all of your commands. This means if you ever give the Come command, you stay put until your dog gets to you and sits. Most people are just so happy their dog came to them, they start praising before their dog actually finishes the command. That's not a bad thing, but you are turning what should be a formal command into a casual command by not making your dog complete the command before releasing her. This is another inconsistency that can cause your dog to test boundaries with your family.

You have to stay put to give your dog that opportunity to sit and complete the command. Often, I see owners say the command, and then start walking away. How will the dog know what to do if you walk away?

> **Postulate:** The Come command is about focus for you, the owner. Teaching the Come command has nothing to do with your dog. It has to do with your understanding of what it means to be specific and consistent.

Overuse of the Come command dilutes its meaning. The Come command is one of the easiest commands to teach, and the hardest to master, not because of the dog, but because the inconsistent way people use the command. Again, the purpose of me teaching this command to an owner is to show them the importance of being consistent and specific with every command and every type of communication with their dog. The more you pay attention to what you are saying, when you are saying it, and what you are communicating in that moment, the better your dog will understand you. Being aware of how you are using the Come command can be great practice for this.

SUMMARY

- Come means to come to you and sit, so you need to stay put while giving the command.
- The Come command is for the owner to focus on being specific.
- Come is used (or misused) as a casual command more than any of the other commands.

DOWN

Oh, the dreaded Down command. This command alone will take up much of your training time. To me, this is the most important command for you and your dog to have the best relationship possible. This command will help your dog find her place in your pack, and hopefully, accept her role there, allowing you to build a fantastic bond.

> **Postulate:** The Down command is *the* most important command you will teach your dog. This is the command where your dog will take its place in your pack, depending on how *willing* she is to do this command.

Down means "lie down." I prefer my dog to be relaxed with a back hip over to one side, although she could instead be in what I call the jet position, where your dog looks like she is ready to jet into a run from the down position. Down is definitely not a belly-rub down.

The Down command is the most important command you will ask your dog to do, and it must be done willingly. Remember, the definition of obedience is the willingness to obey. It is up to you to create this willingness from your dog

The Down command is your first step toward achieving a great bond and trust from your dog. Why is it so important? Because when your dog willingly does a Down command for you, she has accepted her role in your pack. She now depends on you to lead the pack and make sure she is taken care of. She can take on other roles, such as the protector or provider, but she looks to you for what role she is to take in any given situation.

Even though this is a very important command, you should not start by teaching this command. You should work in the progression I outlined at the beginning of this chapter. Why? Because this command is going to be the most challenging of the commands, and it would be a good idea to have a few lessons under your belt before moving into the most difficult area. Those gymnasts you see in the Olympics didn't just run out on the mat and start doing those flips the very first time they ever saw a gym mat.

A Down is the most submissive thing you will ask your dog to do for you. To do the Down command for you, in your dog's head, is her way of accepting her role and accepting you as the pack leader. I put a lot of emphasis on the fact that your dog must do this command *willingly*, because for her to lie down for you, she has to trust you. That is a sign of true dominance on your part. We have talked about the postulate "Dominance is about Trust," in past chapters, and here is where much of that trust happens.

Doing a Down willingly means you ask, and she does. No hesitation, no expectation, and no fear. Your dog cannot expect something from you or fear you when she does the down in order to truly accept her role.

Frequently, I will go into a home, and an owner will tell me that their dog is fully trained, yet they are still having behavior issues. When I do the initial consultation, I ask them to do the commands that their dog knows, then I do the same commands. Sometimes, even if the dog did everything else, the dog will not do the Down command when I am in the room. Sometimes the dog is more likely to do the Down command for me than the owner.

This is when I understand why they are still having behavior issues. The owner has not gained the trust of their dog. If the dog will do the command for me, it is usually because I am so consistent that the dog will quickly pick up that I am serious. Typically, it is not done truly willingly even at that point. I will tell the owner I will work with them, but it will be very important that the dog do this command well.

If there is a motivation involved, such as a treat, I tell them they must get the dog to do all of the commands without treats or any other form of expectation. If a dog expects something from you, is she willing to obey? No.

If a dog lies down for an owner after the owner has yelled at her, or even pushed her down, I just say we are going to have to tweak the Down command until she does it on one command, given in a normal voice, to show she has no fear of the Down command. If a dog lies down out of fear of consequences, is she doing it willingly? Again, no.

When teaching the Down command to an owner, I tell them they are in for about three weeks of training before they get a Down from their dog. The natural progression involves setting a goal of putting the dog into the down position at least 10 times in a workout. The very first week, the owner has to always be in the same position with their dog, they have to always give the Down command in the same place, and they should do a minimum of 10 downs in one workout.

Usually after one week, you will begin to see the frustration. Your dog may start to jump away when you give the command. Your dog might fight you when you try to put her into the down position. Your dog may even get angry and bite you. These are all signs of resistance, and every dog goes through some type of resistance when learning this command. You have to stay on course!

Not all resistance is as blatant as I described above, but most of those things are very normal. There are other signs, and your dog may fall back on, or resist, the other commands she already knows.

I love to get that call halfway through training when the owner says, "My dog forgot EVERYTHING." She didn't forget. She is just challenging you to stay on course. As she resists this command, and as you stay on course, you are slowly taking her control and her level in the hierarchy away. There are much subtler signs of resistance as well. She may start ignoring you when you call her. She may even look away from you when you give the command.

> **Postulate:** All dogs must go through resistance while learning the Down command. This command must be done willingly in order for your dog to accept its place under you in the hierarchy. The Down command is the most submissive command you will ask of your dog.

As you continue to work on the Down command, you will see less of this resistance and more acceptance and obedience in this and other situations. Progress with this command sometimes makes other minor issues, like play-biting, nonthreatening growling at other dogs or animals, and/or humping just go away. When your dog accepts her place, she no longer worries about whether or not you will be the leader. You have now taken that leadership role and she can just be a dog.

As you are teaching the command, allow her to hold the command for longer periods of time. I like to start with 10 to 15 seconds and work up to about three minutes, in 30 second intervals. Letting your dog hold this command allows her to be doing something for you while you are not giving her a lot of attention. Yes, you still need to praise her when she is doing well, but that praise can be dispersed throughout the command sporadically as she holds it longer and longer. Having her hold the command before she actually knows the command also helps her learn what the command is.

> **Postulate:** The key to understanding most commands is to have your dog hold that command for longer periods of time with bigger distractions.

At this point you should not increase the distractions too much. As she learns the command and starts doing the command for you, then you can gradually increase the distractions. You should follow the **Rules of Distraction** that we will discuss in Chapter 4 when adding distraction to your workouts. Also, in the Discover Your Dog Podcast, Episode 038, we discuss the rules in great detail.

SUMMARY

- The Down command is the most important command of the 5 commands we will discuss in this book.
- Down is the most submissive command you will ask your dog to do.
- All dogs have to go through resistance when learning this command.
- The Down command has to be done willingly in order for your dog to fuse well with your family.

On an interesting note, I had a client that was taking one of those retail pet-training classes while training with me. He had asked if he should quit, and I encouraged him continue with the class. I told him to be open to the process, look for what works best for him, and to work through the differences. At one point in the training process (while teaching the Down command), I explained to him what I just wrote above. He said that the trainer in the class said that the Come command was the most important command you should teach your dog.

That floored me. This was very contrary to what I have been training for years. I took a few moments and thought about what his trainer had said, and why they would say that the Come command was more important than the Down command.

In everyday life, I would actually agree. It is more important that your dog come to you when called, rather than lie down when told. If I was teaching a class of basic commands and not teaching how to work on behavior to make a dog part of the family, I would say the same thing.

It is very important that your dog come when called in situations where you need your dog to stay with you, not chase another dog, or come inside. The difference is that if your dog does not accept its place in the pack with you, how could you ever get your dog to the level of trust and obedience you need in those situations? This is how I understand the pack to work, and why I still say an obedient Down command is the single most important training command.

PLACE

Place means for your dog to go to a mat, and lie down on it. I really love this command for a few reasons. First of all, this is a command that starts a progression into intermediate or more advanced training, if that is what you are looking for. You have so many opportunities because of the base this command sets up.

The Place command is a target command. Your dog has to go to the mat, wherever you have laid it on the ground, and lie down on it. You point, and your dog goes and lies down. Once you understand this part of the command, other targets are easy. You could teach your dog the name of every one of her toys and make her get them on command.

The Place command is a multi-layered command. In other words, you will have to break this command into sections in order to teach your dog the whole thing: go to the mat and lie down. Your dog first has to learn to lie down on the mat. This is an important part because sitting, or standing, on the mat is not an option. Once your dog knows that the mat is something to lie down on, she then needs to learn to walk to the mat on her own from a distance away, and lie down in it. This part of the command takes some thought, and the ability to break the command into parts ("Go to the mat" and "Lie down") to train your dog to do the whole thing.

Once I understood that the Place command was multi-layered, I was able to look at anything I might want my dog to do and break that down into parts. I once taught a dog to Stop, Drop, and Roll. I had to break that command down to many parts. I had to teach the dog to stop on command. Then I had to teach the dog the Down command using the word "Drop." Last, I had to teach the dog to roll over. After that, it was just a matter of putting it all together to get her to Stop, Drop, and Roll.

The main reason I like the Place command is because this command, even more than the Down command, is a confidence builder. Once your dog has learned to do the Place command, she will be doing it for you on her own. You should be able to tell your dog to go to her place and she will go, lie down, and stay there until released. You should be able to go on about your business, do things around the house, play Frisbee with your kid, or anything else while your dog stays on the mat.

For a dog that already has a lot of confidence, the Place command solidifies her place in the hierarchy, and she will start to make more of the choices that you want her to make on her own. Your dog will notice that it pleases you for her to stay on the mat and will react the same way when she notices something else that pleases you. The better you are at communicating what choices please you, the better she is at making those choices over and over again just to see your reaction.

> **Postulate:** The Place command is a confidence-building command for your dog. For your dog to hold a command while you do other things helps your dog learn to do for you, even when you are not giving her direct attention.

For an anxious or skittish dog with low confidence levels, the Place command raises her confidence to a much higher level. By holding the Place command, your dog is learning to think for herself and make small choices. When the command is used appropriately, and your dog really trusts you, by going to the place for you and holding the Place command during moments of stress, your dog will start to learn that she is okay when doing what you want her to do. Some anxious behaviors just disappear.

If your dog trusts you, then you will see her act confident in situations during which she may have otherwise been nervous, like greeting people at the door or meeting new people. In those normally nervous situations, your dog will start looking to you on how to behave. Noticing her actions and responding appropriately will give her even more confidence and gain more trust.

My dog, Molly, was terrified of storms. She is a very skittish dog. She has learned that she can relax during storms, and she still looks to me to make sure she is doing good. Fireworks, however, are a whole other story. She still freaks out, and I am there to help her through her freak-out. She looks to me and can eventually relax (to a point) and we get through it together. I do not sympathize with her, I do not scold her; I am just there being the dominant she looks to in those moments. By helping her to establish her place in our family hierarchy, she knows that she can come to me during these times. She is jittery with loud noises, and she does not handle change well, but most people would never know this about her because she shows a lot of self-confidence, especially when she is with me.

SUMMARY

- The Place command is also a target command.
- To teach this command, you have to break it down into two parts.
- The Place command is the confidence-building command.

Now that we have gone through all of the commands and their purpose, let's move forward in training. How do you know your dog is ready for the next step? When do you know your dog has developed the right level of trust? Is your communication creating the behaviors you expect from your dog?

CHAPTER 4

MAKING THE COMMANDS WORK FOR YOU

WHAT ARE YOU COMMUNICATING?

The purpose of my training and this book is to teach you one thing: know what you are communicating at all times! This means, as I have said over and over, you must know what you want, look for your dog to make a choice or react, and then you have to act appropriately.

From this point forward, I am going to talk about how you can use the commands, as well as the tools for training, to help you understand how and why your dog makes the choices and reacts the way she does. The choices may not always be the ones you want, and it will be up to you to be aware of your reactions in every given situation to know what you are teaching your dog in the moment.

Any interaction you have with your dog is a form of communication. This is an important statement for you to understand because, especially if you're committed to training, you should be interacting in some way with your dog every day. Being aware of your dog's actions (or reactions) in those situations tells you what you are communicating in that moment and how you are teaching your dog to behave in the future. Back in Chapter 1 and in the Discover Your Dog Podcast, Episode 040, I discussed a postulate that says, "**Anything you do once or**

twice will not create a behavior." I am going to expand on that, and also introduce another postulate to discuss.

> **Postulate:** It is in your dog's nature to test the boundaries. The more structure you create and the more consistent you are, the less your dog will test the boundaries you have established.

These two postulates are a long jump from each other, yet they work hand-in-hand. The tricky part is catching yourself when you are inconsistent. So many times you will give a command, repeat it, and never realize you have repeated yourself. Your dog knows. Your dog was waiting on that second or third command to react. Your dog was probably waiting for your tone to change to determine if you were serious. Your dog may have even been waiting on the motivation you always give before responding.

There are days when I will open the back door and Oz will just sit there and look at me. Sometimes I just ask, in a normal tone, "Do you want to go out?" He won't move, and I just let the door close. There are days I need him to go out because I know I am going to be out for a long time. This is the time I repeat the question with a firmer tone, then tap my leg. Sometimes he goes, sometimes not. If I really need him to go, I will then say, "Oz, go outside." Now my tone is sharp, not mean, and at this point he will go out. This is the tone I use when I am serious. I am showing the body language that says, "I will not repeat this again." He will get up and go outside.

I know this, because I am aware of my actions and voice tone when I talk to my dogs. This is the part of me that understands what I am communicating at all times. I also see from him that he does not need, nor does he want, to go outside. For the most part, I am going to be okay with that and just let it go.

As the owner, you must start being aware as well. There are some things that you can look for to see if you are having a communication breakdown. How do you feel? When you make a statement or give a command to your dog, and she does not react in the way you want; how do you feel? Are you frustrated? Do you have a strong reaction or quick movements to make your dog do that thing? Or, do you just shrug and realize this is something you need to work on? The last reaction is the best action because you are taking responsibility for the way you are communicating with your dog. The first two reactions are the most common.

If you notice that feeling of frustration or have that strong knee-jerk reaction, it is time to work on what you want your dog to do in that, or a similar, situation. Repeating a command or getting a little louder may seem like it should work, yet when you consistently do that, your dog learns to wait until you reach a certain point before she reacts. You are also now using fear and intimidation (correction) as your training tool. Your dog will either run from you, or do what you want out of fear of what the next action is going to be.

In my rules for training, part one of the **Three Corrections Rule** is that frustration changes your expectations. I teach this because most of you get frustrated with the results (or lack thereof) and do things such as repeat the command, put the dog into position when she knows the command, or just give up entirely. When I teach this rule, it is usually when I have watched you get frustrated with your dog to the point that training is no longer training.

> **Three Corrections Rule – Part 1:** Frustration and anger change expectations. When working with your dog on a command she is learning, once you give three corrections for that command, reach down and put her into that position.

One of the reasons I ended up working on my own was because of the frustration that comes from over-correcting a dog. When correction is used as a method of training, it is only natural that frustration and anger are a part of the training. If a dog is very smart, very stubborn, or both, it becomes a game of wills. Who is the smartest or most stubborn, you or the dog?

When this mental attitude is applied to a corrective method of training, it almost always comes down to who has the strongest will and then becomes physical on your part. To physically "break" a dog might work with a few dogs, and they may be able to bounce back from this, but it definitely does not work with all dogs.

Here is what I mean when I say, "Frustration and anger change expectation." If you give a command that your dog knows well, your expectation should be that your dog does that command within a couple of seconds. If you repeat the command, you have just changed your expectation. No longer did you expect your dog to do what you asked on the first try. If you reach down and put your dog into that position, knowing your dog already knows what to do, again, you have changed your expectations. No longer did you expect your dog to do that command on the first request.

Another thing I see all too often is an owner just giving up. The dog does not respond, or does something different, and then the owner just walks away or changes the command to adapt to what the dog was doing. Again, it is in your dog's nature to test the boundaries. When you know this, you can work through those frustrating moments.

When you are looking for ways to get your dog to pay attention to you in moments of distraction, you are really training. In those moments, you are now the one that is staying on task. You are looking for what you want your dog to do in every given situation, and you are using the motivation and correction tools as they are supposed to be used. You are not getting frustrated or angry and changing what you expect from your dog.

Take your time and *expect* the moments of frustration and anger. Work through them so your dog can get the best part of you. I know that when I get angry, I have lost the battle. I no longer look at what I am doing as a correction or training, I am now just a flurry of emotion. If my dog even responds during that time of emotion, it is very difficult to see and reward her at the moment of choice. I usually just think (or say out loud), "It's about damn time!" That reaction gets you nowhere and your dog learns nothing.

There are other parts to the **Three Corrections Rule**. As you progress through your training, you will understand why and how each of these parts comes into play. Correction is a good and important tool; it just should not be your method of training. By following these rules, you will see that by using correction at the proper level, and in the proper moments, you will be creating great communication. Too often, you want to correct and then don't follow up the correction by getting your dog to make another choice. A good choice. With people, this works because we analyze. Dogs, again, are only reactive, and if you do not follow up a correction appropriately, you will only cause your dog to fear you in a given situation.

> **Three Corrections Rule – Part 2:** The correction needs to get your dog to stop doing what she is doing and pay attention. This means you need to correct to the level that gets her attention. If you correct out of anger, you are probably correcting too hard and chances are, you will not praise once your dog responds to what you asked. If you

correct too softly, then you are not making your dog stop doing what she is doing and pay attention. That would not be considered a correction.

As you see, getting frustrated and angry in a situation does not improve your dog's behavior and means your expectations have changed. You have the power, and sometimes it is important to step away to see how you use it. If you find you are getting overly frustrated with how a workout is going, stop. Put your dog up for a while. Not in a "time-out;" just take a break. Look at how you react to your dog's behavior and make a change. If you are not able to recognize these moments of frustration, you are only building to a moment of big frustration or anger, maybe even one that brings you to the point of giving up on your dog or even giving your dog away. This should never be the option.

TEN TIMES IN A ROW

How will you know your dog is ready for a correction at any level of training? Remember the **Ten to One Rule**. This ratio will play a huge part in training for the rest of your dog's life. Later in this chapter I will discuss one of my theories. I believe a dog does not truly know a command until she has done that command over one thousand times. This is true, and it takes a lot of patience with putting a dog into a position before the dog is truly ready to be corrected. I will not wait until my dog has done something a thousand times before I start correcting her, so how do I know when to start correcting? When my dog has done any **one** thing **10** times in a row, she is ready to move to the next level.

> **Rules of Distraction – Part 1:** Your dog must do any **one** thing **10** times in a row before moving up to the next level of training.

This is a part of the **Rules of Distraction.** What does moving up to the next level mean? Well, it means moving up a notch from where you are at the time.

In other words, if I was teaching my dog to sit, I would ask my dog to sit, then immediately put her into the sit position. At some point, she is going to sit before I actually put her into position. I will give her big praise, release her, then say the command again. If she sits again, great! If not, I will then put her into the position.

During each daily workout, I only do 10 of any single thing I am working on, then I am done. If my dog does all 10 of the sits I asked her to do, in a row, without motivation and without correction, then I am ready to move forward with this command. In this situation, I may be ready to start correcting my dog for the sit command. That is a move forward. In some instances, it may be moving to a more distracting situation, such as doing a workout outside instead of doing it inside. One level forward is enough. Do not try to move outside and start correcting at the same time; this is too much of a forward move.

This is supposed to be fun for you and your dog. If you move forward too fast, it will cause stress on your dog and frustration for you. It is your dog's job to do what she can to distract you (or test the boundaries), so be ready for this. Some dogs are much better at this than others.

DISTRACTIONS IN THREES

Another part of the **Rules of Distraction**, and another good way to recognize your dog is ready to advance to the next level, is the level in which you can work your dog with distractions. If you put your dog into a distracting situation, or you are using an item to distract your dog, you have to assess whether or not that distraction is too much. If, when the distraction is in full effect, your dog continues to break the command, you have to reduce the distraction by removing your dog from that distracting situation or removing the distracting item.

I like to use the main entry door into your home as an example. A knock on the door or the ring of the doorbell are usually extreme triggers to your dog. This is a point of contention with many of my clients. How your dog greets someone at the door is one of the things we covered in the Praise section of Chapter 1, **Tools for Training**. In *Praise Segment 2*, I give an example describing how you would want your dog to greet friends that have come into your home. Typically, the doorbell and the knock are the triggers that got your dog excited in the first place. If this was something you worked on with your dog on a regular basis, the rest of the behaviors may fall into place much easier.

Let's say this is something you would like to work on with your dog. If you put your dog into a command, like Sit or Down, then had someone ring the doorbell, the likely result is that your dog will break the command and run toward the door. This is a highly distracting situation for your dog. Even if you were great at correcting your dog back to the command, the next two times the doorbell rings, your dog is more than likely going to break the command. At this point it is not a battle of wills, it is about assessing whether or not that distraction was too high. In this case, it was clearly too high because your dog broke the command three times.

It's very important to be aware of this. Once your dog has broken that third command, it is time to take a break. This break is so you can assess the trigger, the level of distraction, and how to lower the level of distraction. Someone outside ringing the doorbell with no warning was a huge distraction. What would be a step lower be? Someone outside knocking on the door with no warning? I think that would be too high of a distraction. So, what would the next lower distraction be?

This is a great train of thought to get to the best starter distraction before moving to the next level. It might be a good idea to write all of these levels down, starting at the bottom, and use it as a checklist to get to the level you want. Let's proceed:

1. Someone outside, ringing the doorbell with no warning.
2. Someone outside, knocking on the door with no warning.
3. Someone outside, ringing the doorbell with a warning it was going to happen.
    a. You might have them peek in and tell you when.
4. Someone outside, knocking on the door with a warning it was going to happen.
5. Someone being seen standing in the doorway and ringing the doorbell with no warning.
6. Someone being seen standing in the doorway and knocking on the door with no warning.
7. Someone being seen standing in the doorway, giving a warning, and ringing the doorbell.
8. Someone being seen standing in the doorway, giving a warning, and knocking on the door.
9. Someone inside at the door, ringing the doorbell without a warning.
10. Someone inside at the door, knocking on the door without a warning.

Are you starting to see a pattern? That someone may be a person your dog doesn't know. Next, drop down to a person your dog knows and go through that list. Next, make that person you. If you made that list three times using different people, starting with you, you now have your checklist of 30 steps to complete. And remember, you must get 10 successful events in a row before you are ready to move to the next step. This is another reason training takes a while.

USING DISTRACTIONS WITH A PURPOSE

> **The Rules of Distraction - Part 2:** Whenever you use something as a distraction during a training session, after the session is done, you have to assess whether or not your dog should be able to participate with that item.

There are many things that can be used as distractions when training your dog to hold a command. It could be as simple as moving away from your dog to someone knocking at the door. It is important to know what distractions are being used when teaching your dog to hold commands and how your dog interacts with each particular distraction on a regular basis. This interaction is what I call participation.

Some are items your dog is allowed to interact with and some are not. During a session where you are tempting your dog with these distractions, it is important to know which is which. What can your dog participate with on a normal everyday basis, and what do you want your dog to never participate with on an everyday basis?

Knowing this difference is very important because at the end of a training session you may have to allow your dog to participate with the thing you used as a distraction while training. For example, if your dog loves to chase the tennis ball, and you are working on your dog holding the sit command while throwing the tennis ball, every time your dog gets up you will be correcting her back to the sit. If you go through this often enough and then you never use the ball in a positive way with your dog, your dog will eventually develop a fear of the tennis ball. Your dog will associate correction with you throwing the ball and may stop going after the ball altogether.

Remember, your goal should be that you are correcting and praising in such a way that your dog never fears you. The same should go for normal everyday things that may distract your dog.

Below, I will list a few items that many times are considered big distractions for dogs and separate them into groups of what your dog should and should not participate with on a regular basis.

Should!

Dog Toys: Balls, stuffed dog toys, bones, ropes, frisbees, etc.

You: Sitting down, Standing, Walking, etc.

Any of these things that you use as a distraction when you are training your dog, you must allow your dog to participate with them after the training session. If you were to sit on a chair and your dog breaks a command several times as you sit, then when done with the session, you will sit in the chair and allow your dog to come to you.

The purpose of allowing your dog to participate with this object or person at this time is to let her know that the thing used as the distraction is not the reason she was corrected. The lesson is that your dog learns she was in command at the time and expected to hold that command until released.

Should Not!

Children's Toys: It is up to you to differentiate these toys to your dog.

The Door: The Doorbell, a knock, Opening or Closing, Someone Walking in or out, etc.

The Counters: Food, Activities such as washing dishes or prepping a meal, cabinets opening and closing, etc.

Sitting at the Table: For Dinner, Working, Talking with guests, Guests, etc.

After using any of these things as a distraction, you do not have to let your dog go to or participate with any of these. These are normal daily distractions that your dog is to leave alone anyway.

DAILY WORKOUTS

Each day builds on the last. Each new skill should build on the last as well. It will be very important that you get through a skill to the level of that day before moving on. Since some of the days repeat themselves, it will be very important that you continue the exercise until a skill has been achieved before moving on. As you build with each day, you should start to see the reason behind the day before. Skipping to a new day or skill may be confusing and cause you to misunderstand why you are doing something.

Keep in mind, moving forward is not only for modifying the behaviors as discussed above, but also for moving forward when training commands as well. Again, the rule for moving forward is that a dog does what you are working on 10 times in a row before she is ready to move on to the next skill or level.

I do not believe a dog has totally learned something until she has done it a thousand times. This is a lot. You will see over time that once a dog has done something this many times, it becomes natural. There is no question about the command. Your dog will still test those boundaries depending on whether you are serious or not. You have to set the expectations.

Children are a huge distraction to dogs. For your dog to sit in a situation where a child wants to give her attention is **huge**. There are times when my neighbors come outside when we are out and they just love my Oz, so I don't ever ask him to sit when they are around. Yet, when we first met, they were very intimidated by his size and excitable demeanor. The Sit command was very important in these first few meetings so he would not scare the children and set a bad example.

He would do the Sit very willingly, looking at me the whole time, just waiting to get attention and be released. He wanted to do this for me because I have taught him that the end results are worth it. He did the Sit willingly, not out of fear or expectation. The results are not the reason he did the Sit; he has just learned that doing the commands willingly is a very positive and loving experience.

> **Postulate:** A dog does not truly know a command until she has done that command over 1,000 times on her own, with no prompting (motivation or correction) from the owner.

This is, yet again, another reason training takes a while. You are looking for the perfect dog from the moment you get your dog. Unfortunately, they don't all come packaged that way. It is up to you to put in the work. The work comes with looking for things for which to praise your dog, not so you have the perfect dog. My dogs still get praised for going potty outside. Both my dogs are potty-trained, but I still praise them because I always want them to potty outside.

One thousand times seems daunting, yet in the lifetime of your dog, it isn't that much. With early instruction, consistency, and dedication to your dog, you can reach that number very quickly. It takes practice and awareness.

Don't give up. Or, to put it in the affirmative, keep going even when it gets frustrating and you think you are not progressing. Many times, I go into a home and the owner tells me that their dog is not progressing. When I take the leash and do the lesson, the dog does everything I asked the owner to teach their dog that week. Usually that frustrates the client even more. My statement to them, and to you, is "The only reason your dog is doing this well for me is because you were doing the work." If you don't do the work, you will get no results. Why did the dog do so great for me? Because I am extremely consistent; your dog does not know if she can test the boundaries with me, and I am impeccable with my timing. As you practice, you will get better with this timing as well. The better you are with your timing, the better you will feel about your training, and the better your dog will do for you as well.

> **Postulate:** When you have a great attitude, no matter what the situation, you will always see better results because you are looking for and expecting better results.

I compare learning to communicate with your dog to learning a new language. The better you get, the more confidence you gain to try new things. Not only are you learning how to work with and teach your dog, you are also learning to understand your dog better. You will begin to see more and more signs from your dog that give you information. You will see when your dog is really happy (most people believe they can see this already), when your dog is sad or depressed, and when your dog really needs something from you. There are times that I could tell when my dog was in pain or did not feel good, just by the way she would walk toward me. It just wasn't normal. I have never seen this in dogs with which I haven't developed a bond.

Most of the time, it takes a dog about six months to learn you. During this time, your dog is testing all types of boundaries. How you respond is how your dog learns what she can and can't do. Are you consistent? What are your limits? When are you serious or not? What can your dog push you to do that you would normally not do?

These are the things she is looking for when you start your relationship. How does a dog learn and know these things? There are many ways. The two main ways are your body language and your tone of voice.

> **Postulate:** Dogs pick up on your body language before they pick up on any other mode of communication from you. It usually takes a dog about six months to learn and really understand your body language.

During this introductory period, you are giving your dog a lot of information. When you yell but don't follow through with making your dog do a command, you have shown her she does not have to do what you said all the time. When you correct your dog long after she has done something, you are communicating that whatever she is doing right at that moment of correction is the wrong thing. When you correct your dog for a behavior during certain times and then let her get away with it at other times, you are showing her you are inconsistent and sending the message that it is okay to test the boundaries.

CHAPTER 5

BEING ON PURPOSE WITH TRAINING

LEAVE THE LEASH ON YOUR DOG!

You should be working with your dog for the next 10 to 12 weeks if you are doing basic obedience training. During this time, you should have the leash on your dog. I recommend a five to six-foot training lead that is comfortable to the grip. I also recommend a good collar that your dog cannot slip out of. In the Discover Your Dog Podcast, Episode 027, I talk about such collars and the reasons why your training collar should not also be your dog's ID collar.

The leash is your best training tool for everyday use. The main reason is so that you can correct your dog (make her stop doing what she is doing and pay attention to you) without touching your dog. Back in Chapter 1, the **Tools for Training**, I talked about how important touch was to your dog. If you have to touch your dog, especially when correcting your dog, then you are sending a mixed message. This is where a leash comes in handy. You also communicate much better when you can make your dog pay attention to you.

> **Postulate:** When leash training, leaving the leash on your dog creates a sense of control whether you are touching the leash or not.

Ever notice that when you have the leash on your dog she is paying better attention and minding better? This is because of what that leash represents to your dog: physical control. You may not have physical control at all times, and yet, the few times you were able to catch your dog, you corrected your dog in the moment of a behavior, or you could get your dog to follow an instruction in the moment; your dog started to associate that leash with that control. I have seen many dogs get upset with the leash instead of getting upset with the trainer that just gave a correction. This is another great use of the leash as a training tool.

Most clients want to get to the off-leash part of training as soon as we start. Many clients will tell me how well their dog behaved off the leash during the training process. My response is always the same: We don't do off-leash training. I will also tell a client that it takes over a year to get a dog fully off-leash trained. Later in this chapter, I will be going over the stages to off-leash training, and you will see why I say it takes over a year.

For now, be resigned to the fact you should always have the leash on your dog when you are with her. If you are leaving your dog alone or putting her in a crate, take it off. If the leash is so long that it gets caught on things when your dog is running around the house, cut it short or get a tab. A tab is a short leash made for keeping your dog close. If your dog is chewing, peeing on, or just generally abusing the leash, you may have to get creative. I have had to use a short chain for dogs that chew the leashes off. I have bought cheap leashes from Goodwill for dogs that chew on them or drag them through everything. I have even had to hand-make a short leash from rope that could be easily replaced. I have also had to buy washable leashes because the dog would constantly go to the bathroom on it.

You can be as creative as your environment allows. There are leashes at my back door and front door. With a new dog, I will put on an outside leash, then change to an inside leash when they are ready to come inside. Often, I go into a new owner's home, and they don't even have a good leash. If you don't have the proper tools to work with your dog, you will be setting you and your dog up for failure from the beginning.

TIMING OF CORRECTION AND PRAISE

Timing is everything. This is especially true when it comes to dog training. Timing is so important because your dog is reactive. Your dog will not take the time to analyze why that pillow was worth destroying, knowing that she is going to get in a lot of trouble later. If this was the case, we would call them children, not dogs.

Being that your dog is reactive, you also have to be reactive with your corrections and your praises. To be effective, that reaction (correction or praise) must be delivered when your dog is in the act (or right after).

> **Postulate:** Correcting your dog long after a behavior you don't want, or away from the location of the infraction, does not make sense to her. That correction has nothing to do with the past behavior and your dog thinks what she is doing at the time of the correction is why she is getting corrected. You have about a five-second reaction time once you see a behavior you want to correct. Any amount of time beyond that is too late.

The Discover Your Dog Podcast, Episode 051, title is "Catch Your Dog Red-Handed or Forget It!" That is the essence of a correction. If you don't catch your dog in the act, you have nothing to correct. As a matter of fact, it is your fault. If there is anyone that needs correcting after the fact it is you, the owner, for giving your dog too much freedom. One of the most frustrating things to hear as a dog trainer is an owner that refuses to keep a close watch on their dog as a puppy (or when they first get a new dog, puppy or not) and has the expectation that the dog should "just know!" If you cannot be consistent with the rules, how is a dog supposed to "just know?"

Catching your dog in the act and giving an appropriate correction in the moment makes your dog stop doing what she is doing and pay attention to you. At that moment, you have a couple of choices to make. You walk away knowing that you just communicated your wish for your dog to stop that behavior, or you praise your dog. You should understand that each reaction communicates something different for your dog and that those are the only two choices you should make after making a well-timed correction.

CORRECTING AFTER THE FACT

Correcting your dog well after she has done something you don't want is not effective correction. Mentally, most dogs have about a five to 15-second short-term memory span. I personally think it is much shorter than that; I just give them the benefit of the doubt. This is why you will see a dog go from one thing to the next very quickly. If you ever saw the movie *Up*, I call it the "Squirrel" factor. I have heard people refer to it as the "Shiny Objects" behavior. A dog is not only easily distracted, but she will also move to another behavior or action very quickly when stressed.

Because of this rapid attention-changing process, correcting in a timely manner is very important. If you wait too late, or correct when you find the infraction, what you are really correcting for is the behavior your dog is doing at that moment. Even if you bring your dog to the scene of the crime, your dog has no idea that crime scene represents.

Let's say you and your dog are enjoying some couch time. You get up to get something out of the kitchen and notice that your dog has gotten into the trashcan. You go back into the living room, pick up your dog, and take her into the kitchen. All this time, you are walking and talking angrily. Your dog will think she is in trouble for being on the couch or lying where she was. She will associate all the bad energy from you for what she is doing right then. She forgot about the trashcan a long time ago. If you take her to the trashcan and spank her, you are now making that scene a bad scene as well, and she is just associating being picked up by you as bad. Now, for the most part you may pick up your dog nicely and give sweet vibes when you do, and for the most part she will want to be picked up by you. Yet, there will be times when she is very hesitant about being picked up or may even walk away from you when you call her because you are very close to that body language and voice tone she recognizes as being in trouble.

Your body language and voice tone are what she is responding to when you think "she knows" what she did wrong. Really, when you see that duck (what I refer to as the "just got beaten" look) or the guilty look, your dog is just trying to figure you out in the moment. If you ever want to test that theory, whenever you see that look, quickly change your energy to happy and joyful and see what happens with your dog, even if you see something that you consider a bad behavior. Changing your energy and attitude is very difficult for most people to do, and that is why you recognize this look as an "I am guilty" look from your dog.

ANTICIPATION AND AVOIDANCE TRAINING

Knowing the level at which your dog is trained is very important. It is helpful when thinking about whether you should wait on your dog to make a choice or go ahead and correct for the hesitation. This anticipation goes two ways. Sometimes, you anticipate your dog will do something wrong and correct for that thing before it happens. Other times, you anticipate that your dog is going to do a command you ask and you wait too long for the action instead of giving a timely correction.

In Chapter 1, **Tools for Training**, I discussed why correction is not a good method of training. One reason was that over-correcting your dog creates fear. One way to really create fear from your dog is to correct too quickly and too harshly. You may anticipate what your dog is going to do, rather than give your dog a choice. In this case, you gave an unnecessary correction. Again, timing is very important. When you have control of the leash, and your dog is in a situation where she can make a choice, let her. Once she has made the choice, you then have the choice to praise or correct in the moment.

This does not mean you should wait a long time before making a correction. The pause should be to the level at which your dog knows a command. If your dog knows to sit when you stop in the Heel command, you can correct a little sooner than you would if your dog is just learning that command.

The most common example is walking on-leash. If you are walking your dog, working on that loose leash walk, and you see a potential distraction ahead, there is a tendency to cinch up on the leash. You have anticipated that your dog will be distracted by that thing, and you took measures against that. The distraction should be looked at as a training opportunity. By tightening the leash prior to the distraction, you have taken that opportunity away. By the time your dog does pull or get distracted, you have already started the process of correction.

I call this **Avoidance Training**. If you avoid a situation, you will never get your dog to understand a choice can be made. It also gives you, the owner, an out because you don't have to look for what you want. You just avoid what you don't want.

Other examples of avoidance training are having a tight leash on your dog when greeting people, putting up a gate or barrier to another room in the house, and even having a fence or gate on your property. All of these types of avoidance allow you to not have to think or work with your dog on what you expect your dog to do in each of the situations. For example, you may never work on your dog learning to stay in your yard because of that fence. One day someone leaves the gate open, and your dog gets out and runs away. Even though that fence sounded like a good idea at the time, it was just a way for you to get out of the work it would take to make your dog want to stay on your property.

When do you know you have corrected enough versus too much? Your dog can and will give you many stress signs. I will go into a few of them here, but I will not go into a big explanation. I have been training dogs for over 15 years as of the time of this book. The stress signs I see are very different with different dogs and in different situations. The fact is, stress signs could be a combination of many things. If I were to tell you one or two things I know could be a stress sign, it may or may not be the same thing that happens in the next stressful situation. If you start looking for that particular sign all the time, you will see it and think your dog is stressing out all the time.

I suggest you do further research if you think you are over-stressing your dog. In order to move forward, some stress has to happen. It is through stress and struggle that changes are made.

One obvious sign is excessive yawning. One or two yawns may be a sign that your dog is getting to the point or that she is tired.

Another sign is your dog licking her chops. Sometimes this may sound like teeth chattering and sometimes you see your dog excessively licking around the lips and nose. Again, if the dog is over-stressed this action may be done excessively, but just because your dog is licking around her lips does not necessarily mean she is stressed. It could mean she got something on her face or she smells something good. The last stress sign that I consider an obvious stress sign is over-scratching, especially when a command has been given. This is not just a sign of stress; it is a sign of avoidance from your dog as well.

Don't over-think these signs. Again, look for signs and work through them. This is what I mean by being aware of your dog's behavior in the moment and when you are being purposeful with your dog training.

CORRECTING WITH PURPOSE

When you are correcting with purpose, you are correcting to get your dog to stop doing what she is doing and pay attention in the moment. That is it! Part 3 of my **Three Corrections Rule** covers what correcting with a purpose means.

> **Three Corrections Rule – Part 3:** If your dog knows a command, and you still have to correct three times or more to get your dog to do that command, you are not using the tools properly. It is up to you to practice and increase your dog's willingness to do a certain command. You should only correct to the level you need to get your dog's attention, and you should practice praising for doing that command more often. Motivation can be used, and it is up to you to be aware when your dog starts to expect that motivation.

Your correction should make your dog stop doing what she is doing and pay attention. If you find yourself getting angry or frustrated when, or right after, correcting your dog, you have lost control. The third part of the **Three Corrections Rule** is about you being efficient and effective with your corrections and never getting angry. I watch people give four, five, six, or more corrections and get louder, angrier, and more frustrated with each correction. The point is to make a correction that gets your dog's attention, not to hurt your dog. Some people never get to that level, because they never change the tone or focus on each of the half-dozen corrections. The point here is lost because the level of correction never changes.

Neither of the above scenarios is effective. One is too harsh and the other too light. A proper correction should be done in three corrections or less. The same goes with motivation. You should always choose to motivate your dog over correction when the choice can be made. Timing is important, and you have to be aware of the level of distraction and motivation you need when making that choice.

> **Rule:** Always choose motivation over correction when there is a choice. When you are using motivation as a tool, your dog is more likely to remember the command and more likely to want to do that command.

If you can motivate your dog to look at you, turn a corner with you, or pay attention during a big distraction, you are going to get better results in the long run. The more times your dog finishes a command after being motivated, the more likely your dog is to do, or want to do, that command again. Again, it comes down to timing and levels of motivation. Review the section on **Motivation** in the **Tools for Training** chapter.

TIMING YOUR PRAISE

As important as it is to time your corrections, it is even more important to time your praise. Praise is the only way you teach and train your dog to do what you want. The problem is not that you don't see the things you want your dog to do; the problem is that you see them, but you are not willing to praise because you think it's just what your dog is supposed to do all the time. When your dog is doing something she is supposed to do, it is common to just ignore that behavior because we are taught as humans that doing what you are supposed to do is not worthy of praise. The only thing worthy of praise is when someone goes over and above the "call of duty." This is what gets noticed. In the corporate world, this is what gets a person promotions and recognition. As humans, it is not enough to do just what is necessary to get by unless you just want to stay status quo all of your life.

In dog behavior and communication, this is not the case. You need to recognize every time your dog is doing what you want in order to really teach your dog. Again, as I have said throughout this book, your dog is reactive. This means if you react, respond, give attention to, and/or praise when your dog is doing the simplest thing you want her to, you will be teaching your dog to do that thing. Your dog needs that reaction from you to learn.

This is where that all-important timing of praise comes in. Not only do you have to notice your dog is doing what you want, you have to praise at the time of choice or reaction. Often, I see a person walking down the street with their dog and there is never any positive attention when their dog is walking loose on the leash. When you make the choice to praise during those moments, you give attention to what you want instead of just reacting to behaviors you don't want.

In that same scene with the person walking their dog, when a distraction arrives, then the owner starts to give attention. Even if it is negative attention, it is still attention for that reaction and to the dog, it is praise.

There are other things you may be doing to praise your dog that you have no idea you are doing. In Chapter 1, **Tools for Training**, I talked about touch being the biggest form of praise you can give your dog. There are two things you need to watch for when training. One, is your dog touching you? If you are letting your dog touch you during a session, you are touching. That touch, even though you are not the one initiating it, is giving praise for whatever your dog is doing at the time. If you say "Sit" and your dog continues to stand, touching your leg, you are allowing the praise to happen. Step away.

The second thing you need to watch for is eye contact. Eye contact with a dog is one of two things: praise or a challenge. Since this is your dog and you have had her awhile, you are rarely, if ever, challenging your dog when you look at her. She knows you by now. That means the eye contact is a form of praise.

> **Postulate:** Looking your dog in the eyes is one of two things: praise or a challenge. As an owner, you are never challenging your dog, ever. To look your dog in her eyes at the moment she is doing anything is praising her for that thing.

Again, this means if you ask your dog to lie down and she is looking you in the eye while sitting, you are praising her for continuing to sit. Look away. Be aloof. Don't stop watching your dog, just let her know, by breaking the eye contact, and maybe even giving a sign like crossing your arms, that you are not going to give her any attention until she does what you tell her. That aloofness can be a strong tool, especially if you have a dog that really wants to please you.

You may notice that your dog might do the same to you. I have seen many dogs look in another direction when given a command. I have also noticed dogs look away when spoken to in a tone they don't like. For the most part, you think your dog should be looking at you all the time when you are communicating. This is not the case. This is why your dog won't look at you. She knows, "If I don't look at him, I don't have to do what he says." Of course, your dog is not analyzing and thinking in those terms. Your dog has just learned through your reactions that this is the case.

CONTROL

What is control? If I was to walk into your home and tell you your dog was in control of you, what would you think? Most people say it means that their dog is in charge, but to me, being in charge and being in control are a little bit different.

It is up to you to notice if you or your dog is in charge. Below, I am going to discuss what my theory is in dog training when it comes to control. This theory is based on actions your dog may take during a training session or in everyday life. Your dog has no idea she is doing these things to take control, but the more you allow her to continue, the more your dog will test you in other areas of your life.

For you to have control means you must be confident about what you are communicating at all times, and you also must be confident about what you are interpreting from your dog. Too many times that interpretation comes from what you think as a human. Hopefully, you are learning that dogs do not think the same way.

> **Postulate:** Control is about confidence. Confidence comes from knowing what you are communicating in every given situation. Once you are aware of your communication, you are going to naturally be consistent.

Who is in control when it comes to your dog's behaviors? You will make mistakes when you are communicating with your dog. The mistakes aren't the things you need to worry about; the consistent behavior on your part is. Are you doing the same things over and over and expecting a different result? Are you even aware you are doing those same things over and over? In the **Tools for Training** chapter, I talk about my postulate: Anything you do once or twice does not create a behavior. The same goes for stopping a behavior. The problem arises when you do not realize you are doing the same thing over and over.

When I talk about control, I talk about it in just that way: To make confident decisions you must be aware you are making those choices or decisions. I am very confident in how I communicate with all dogs. I approach, react, interact, and introduce myself to dogs using certain body languages and voice tones without thinking about what I am doing at the time. I can describe everything I did after the interaction, yet I did not think about it when I was doing it. This is confidence. This is control.

There are many things dogs do to take control as well. One example that happens very often in training situations I call "Down Happy." When a dog finally gets the Down command, there is a tendency for a dog to get "down happy." In other words, your dog may just go straight to lying down when you do a Heel or Come. Remember, she is supposed to sit at the end of either of those commands. By going into the Down, your dog is taking control of the workout. When I tell this to a client, they don't believe it until I have them put their dog in a proper sit and then ask their dog to do the Down command. When they ask their dog, the dog will hesitate or refuse altogether to do the Down. Why? Because the dog is no longer in control. I even point out how the dog was so willing to lie down on its own as if it was anticipating the next command, yet when the owner gave the command she refused.

The interesting part is the dog had no clue it was taking control. In human terms, if you have to bribe someone to help you, if you get angry at something, or if someone you are working with quits, you were not in control. The person you had to bribe, you got angry at, or the on that just quit was the one in control. That person, more than likely, did not have the intent of being in control. They just did what they wanted on their terms, not yours. This action is not usually premeditated, it is done unconsciously.

The same goes for your dog, yet when she makes those decisions more and more often and gets away with it, she is taking control. By allowing those actions, you are losing control and other behaviors start to show as a result. This is one reason why I say in the **Tools for Training** chapter that you cannot fix many behaviors until your dog does the Down command willingly.

USING THE "ALL DONE" COMMAND

Rule: "All Done" means your dog is finished with the last command you gave. Use this command throughout your workout. Usually, the novice trainer will only use this command at the end of the entire workout or while praising for completing a command. This causes your dog to think she is done with the workout entirely and/or that praise is also a release.

This takes practice. The typical response to the All Done command from an owner is to take the leash off the dog. This teaches the dog that nothing else has to be done from the moment she heard the command "All Done." You want your dog to learn that she is just complete with the last thing you told her.

Using the All Done command appropriately helps in many ways. One, it releases your dog from a command when you are no longer able (or willing) to pay attention to her in a distracting situation. In other words, if your dog is too distracted, and there is no point in trying to get her to do a command, just say "all done." This releases your dog. Later, you can work to get her through that distraction.

Another purpose for the All Done command is so you don't have to say the word, "Stay."

> **Rule:** Stay is incorporated in all commands and does not need to be said. Your dog is released when you say "All Done."

When you have a release command such as All Done, stay becomes a wasted word. If you say "stay" and you still have to release your dog, you have not taught your dog that the command was meant to be held until released. If you tell your dog to sit, she should hold that command until you release her. If you tell your dog to sit and then you have to say "stay," what was the purpose of just saying sit? Again, it comes to being specific when you give your dog a command.

WHAT YOUR DOG KNOWS

Frequently, I go into a home well after a dog has been established in the household. I would love it if you were required to hire me before ever getting a dog. Many problems would be completely eliminated if owners either took on the responsibility of learning about their new dog or were required to take a class.

Seeing how it is not required, many issues do arise. One thing I will tell an owner that just got a new dog or puppy is that it takes six months for a dog to learn you. During those months, your dog learns when you are serious and when you are not serious by your body language and voice tone. Your dog is also testing the boundaries to see how far she can push the limits and the level at which you are willing to correct or reward certain behaviors. This is all reactive learning. As stated previously, dogs pick up on your body language before they pick up on any other mode of communication from you.

Many factors come into play during this first six months, which is why many people don't call me until something has reached a breaking point. Your dog is testing the boundaries from the beginning. Your dog is finding out if you are going to be consistent in each and every situation, at what level you will give in to her persistence, and whether or not she can be higher in the hierarchy than each member of your family. This first six months is the time to create the structure, or rules, in your home.

Another reason I would love to come into a home prior to a family getting a new dog is that humans have very different personalities, even within one family. There are other human variances to note: Age, health, size, willingness, and ability to communicate, to name a few. Because of all of these factors and the combinations that could make up a family, it's beneficial to know what breed of dog may work best.

> **Postulate:** Humans have personalities. Because of this, you will find that different people react very

differently in many situations. This includes members of the same family as well as people of different sexes, ages, races, and personal backgrounds.

People have differing beliefs on how dogs should be raised as well. Just the fact that you are reading this book shows you want to take responsibility and learn more about how to make your dog a great part of your family. As Devin says in every podcast episode, you want "to demystify your dog's behavior so you can get the best out of dog training."

The reason you want to figure out what breed works best in your family is almost the same as the postulate above. Dogs have personalities. For the most part, dogs of the same breed carry many of the same traits, although this does not hold true in every case.

Postulate: Dogs have personalities. Because of this, you will find that different dogs react very different in many situations. This includes dogs of the same breed.

If you were to prescreen your family and the dog's breed, you still do not have a 100% guarantee that everything is going to be perfect. Many things can go undetected at an early age, and many times, people change their attitudes about a dog. Dogs are a lot of responsibility. Do your best. Prescreening only gets you a better start than just jumping in feet first. Most people (and I mean almost everyone) jump in feet first, then worry about the problems later.

That is okay, too. It's why I am in business. Personalities clash. My job, and what I hope you take away from this book, is to bridge that gap. In the podcasts and in this book, we are "creating the groundwork" for you to have better communication and to build a better relationship with your dog.

CASUAL VS FORMAL COMMANDS

There are a few more things I would like to discuss before going into the final stages of training in this book. Everyone wants to do all the commands and to have to best-behaved dog off the leash as well as on the leash. I know this, because the majority of the time I go into a client's home, they tell me everything they have done off the leash and how well their dog is doing. For you, the dog owner, there are steps that must be taken to be successful in your off-leash journey.

I have noticed there are commands you will use that are formal and there are things you say in a casual way to your dog. It is good to know this difference. It is also good to know when and why you should use these commands. The Heel command is a good example. Let's discuss the Heel command first, then I will list a few other things you may say to your dog in a formal versus casual way.

We discussed the Heel command in great detail in the Training Progression chapter. Heel is a very formal command that means "Walk at my left side and sit when I stop." Heel should only be used in formal situations such as workouts or competitions. Heel is not something to do while you are taking your dog for a walk. For your dog to be in the Heel command when you walk means she cannot pee, sniff, or walk on any side except your left. How fun would that be for you and your dog? Not very fun at all.

When I train people, I suggest a casual command, "Let's Go." Let's Go only means that you, the owner, are moving. This means that when you say "Let's go," you have to **move**. The Let's Go command is only about you, not your dog. By saying "Let's go," you are telling your dog you are moving. Since your dog is on the leash, she will have to come with you at some point or you will be pulling her. If your dog wants to stop to sniff, visit, or pee on something, then you have two choices: Let your dog stop and you stop with her, or tell your dog, "No, Let's Go" and keep moving. In this casual command, you can stop and go as often as you want because you are only telling your dog when you are moving, not expecting her to move with you or that she has to be at your side.

Below are some other things you may use as casual versus formal commands in your everyday life. I have worded these as what I use, but you may prefer your own wording. The wording is not important, the intent is. Are you being casual or formal when you speak to your dog?

Casual	Formal
Let's Go	Heel
Go to Bed	Place
Cute Pet Name	Your Dog's Full Name
Come On	Come
Get Down	Down

I call my dogs Ma or Ozzer when I am talking to them casually. I call them Molly or Oz when I am being formal and want them to listen. It's not just in the wording, it is also in the tone I use when talking to them. Your dog should know the difference between when you are giving a command or just speaking casually. Using your voice tone with intention and knowing the difference takes practice. A good reference or follow-up to this section would be to listen to the Discover Your Dog Podcast, Episode 031, "How to Use Formal vs Casual Commands with your Dog."

BEHAVIORS TO STOP VS BEHAVIORS TO NEVER DO

Sometimes there are behaviors you may be okay with; you may just want your dog to stop doing that behavior when told. The difference between correcting a behavior you are okay with and stopping a behavior you are not okay with is something I talk about in all of my training sessions, yet I don't know if most people really get and understand the difference. I have even come up with a way of correcting differently for either of these behaviors so there is a distinction. It is not really complicated. You have a tendency to be vague on what you want from their dog. Vague language is confusing and inconsistent when communicating with your dog.

Barking is an example of a behavior to stop. Most people are okay with their dogs barking to alert them of something. In other words, if a friend came into your house unannounced, you may be okay if your dog barked, but you would want her to be quiet when you told her. Your corrective word could be "Hush!"

In most cases, people that come into your home or that you greet on the street are people who are friendly, and you want your dog to be friendly with them. Even when another dog comes to visit you and your dog, you typically know the dogs and people involved. In these cases, you may not want your dog to bark incessantly. When you want the barking to stop, you should use a word or phrase in a corrective tone. If your dog stops, you should praise your dog immediately. This is the key difference to communicating a behavior you want your dog to stop when told, versus correcting for a behavior you never want your dog to do.

By praising your dog after giving a correction, or saying a corrective phrase, you are telling your dog that she was okay doing what she was doing, she just has to stop when told. In this case, since what you want is the behavior to stop, you are praising at the correct moment.

Here is the twist. If you praise your dog for stopping a behavior you did not want in the first place, such as counter surfing, then you are telling her it was okay to counter surf as long as she got down when told.

> **Postulate:** If there is a behavior you are okay with in general, but would like your dog to stop doing when told, correct with a word or phrase then immediately praise her for doing what you asked. This shows her it was okay to do that thing, but she should stop when told.

If it is a behavior you never want your dog to do, you correct with a 'No' then you immediately walk away or take your dog away from the situation with no attention afterwards. The goal here is to get your dog to understand that is something you never want her to do, so you cannot give her attention right after the correction. Let your dog have time to react to the correction on her own.

Below are two lists. One list is behaviors you may be okay with but want your dog to stop when told, along with suggested corrective words or phrases.

Behaviors to Stop!	Corrective Word/Phrase
Barking	Hush!
Getting on furniture	Get off!
Something in the mouth	Drop it!
Jumping up	Get down!

Pulling toward something	Easy!

Remember to immediately praise if the behavior stops right after the corrective words.

The second list is behaviors you may not want your do to ever do along with the suggested corrective word. As you will see, that word should always be "No."

Behaviors to Never Do!	Corrective Word
Jumping up	No!
Play biting	No!
Counter surfing	No!
Lunging on-leash	No!
Running out the door	No!

Remember to immediately walk away or ignore your dog after the corrective word.

STARTING THE OFF-LEASH PROCESS

You think you are ready? I know you want this! I know you want your dog to do everything off the leash that she will do on the leash. Believe it or not, this whole book is geared toward getting you to this point. No one showed me what to do after my dog was totally trained on-leash. I took no advanced classes, and the ones offered in Nashville were high in treats and motivation as the tool for teaching more advanced and off-leash skills. My dog wasn't trained with treats prior to learning off-leash commands, so I did not know how incorporating them into the training at this point was going to work. What I did learn about dogs is that the more they valued a treat or toy, the easier it was to get them to do many things off the leash because of that high expectation. One of my dogs, Molly, does not care much about toys and would rarely take a treat from your hand. I have even watched her take a dog biscuit and bury it for later. It was not an immediate motivation to her.

What I learned is that true off-leash training meant my dog had to do what I wanted willingly. This is when I started to truly understand what obedience was—the willingness to obey. Your dog has to want to do what you ask and expect her to do.

It all circles back to the beginning. If we were not focusing on that simple definition from the beginning, we would not be able to get to this point at all. The focus must always be on the definition of obedience. When you have a full understanding of that, everything else falls into place. Why? Because you have to look for what you want, you have to react in a positive, pleasing way when your dog does the thing you wanted (with good timing), and you have to correct appropriately for what you don't want (with good timing). Then, and only then, will you be creating a willingness to obey from your dog.

THREE STAGES FOR OFF-LEASH TRAINING

STAGE ONE

On-Leash: This is a two to three-month process, and everything is done on-leash. This is the process you should have been going through while reading this book. When I am training a new client, this is how long it typically takes to train their dog. Take the time and be patient. Or, if these statements work better for you: be more stubborn than your dog, be more insistent than your dog, and/or be more aware than your dog.

You keep your dog on the leash because you want to have physical control of your dog during times of learning. If you tell your dog to sit and she keeps running away, you have no control and the training is going to take much longer. The leash is a physical tool that helps you to work with your dog and get to the second stage much faster.

The first part of training is teaching your dog to associate specific words with specific meanings. In the **Training Progression** section of this book, I gave you the definition of each command. These definitions are very specific. If you teach your dog to lie down, the command is Down. This means for your dog to lie down, all the way on the ground. If you give this command and your dog resists lying down for you, you need to have a way of physically keeping her near you so you can put her into that position. You will have to put her into the down position many times before she does it on her own the first time.

STAGE TWO

Not Touching the Leash: This is a four to five-month process where you will start the **Three Rules of Consistency.** You will be asking your dog to do commands while still on the leash, but without you touching your dog or the leash once you have given a command.

This is the beginning of the off-leash process. The reason you keep your dog on the leash is that during the first stage the leash started to represent something to your dog. By now, you should have noticed that your dog behaves much better on the leash than off the leash, even when you aren't touching the leash. This is a benefit of the on-leash training you have been doing this whole time.

When beginning this stage, you are starting the process of teaching yourself to be specific and consistent. You are also beginning the process of teaching your dog to want to do things for you. To be obedient. To be willing to obey!

STAGE THREE

Off-Leash: This is a six to seven-month process, and you will now start asking your dog to do commands with no leash at all.

Truly off-leash. This is the moment you have been waiting on. Before starting this process, you should be seeing great results from your **Stage Two** work. If you need to, review the sections on **Making the Commands Work for You**. You must continue following the **Ten to One Rule** and the **Rules of Distraction** to really know if your dog is ready to advance to this level. Trust yourself and trust your dog. It takes a lot of work and time. You will create an amazing bond and relationship by being honest with yourself and doing the work it takes. It does take a year or more to have a very well-trained off-leash dog. If you do it right, you have many, many years of fun and trust with your dog. So, do it right. Also, if you have been diligent with your homework and you have reached this point at the appropriate time, you never have to go back or redo anything. Yes, there may be setbacks, but isn't life full of them, anyway? One of my favorite sayings is:

> **"Stumbling blocks are reroutes to a better destination."**

That saying is what being aware is about. It is about noticing what got in the way and making a change. That change will lead to a much better result, especially when it comes to training and communicating with your dog.

THREE RULES OF CONSISTENCY

Before I go into these rules, you need to know a few things. One is that these rules are geared toward working your dog off the leash. Also, almost everything I do is in threes, just like I have done throughout the book. I want things to be simple. I need things to be simple. If I can break something down or divide it into three parts, to me, that is a simpler way to do that thing. Because of this I have the **Three Tools for Training** (Praise, Motivation, and Correction) and I have the **Three Stages to Off-Leash Training** as we discussed prior to this section. Now you are going to learn my **Three Rules of Consistency**. Many of my rules are also broken down into three parts as well.

Another thing is that I stay true to the **Ten to One Rule** that I have discussed throughout the book. Remember, for every one time you correct your dog for anything, you have to praise her ten times for making the choice you want.

Lastly, these rules are about *you*; they have nothing to do with your dog. Throughout your training and especially in this section of the book, I have been teaching you how to behave, not your dog.

When I explain each rule below, I am talking about what you need to be doing, not your dog. Even though I say this and emphasize this fact to clients, when I give scenarios on how each of the rules work the client still relates the mistakes and hesitations to their dog.

> **Rule Number One:** Whenever you give a command, no matter what happens, you always have to end it in a positive way.

Rule Number One is the most important rule!

There are two things that come up when I tell this rule to an owner for the first time. One is that it is very important to know why this is the most important rule. The other is to understand what it means to end a command in a positive way.

We have talked about my theories as to why and how dogs remember throughout this book. One thing I realized is that I want my dog to behave as well, or better, off the leash as she does on the leash.

Molly was that first dog that taught me the lessons I now teach. The reason I say that obedience is the willingness to obey is because when I first learned to train with Molly, I did not have this definition in mind. When I started letting her off the leash to make choices on her own, the methods that I had learned were not working to make her want to do what I expected of her. Yes, she was loving and loyal, but there were many times she would just wander off, and I would get so upset with her. I would correct her, scold her, and even make her hold commands for extensive times. Nothing worked. If anything, she would see me coming with that angry look and run. It was very frustrating.

Finally, I started to make a shift in my mentality. When I did that, along with the years I have had to practice my theories, I came up with rules, postulates, and definitions that would fit my style of training. I have never seen the total package in writing until now.

Why end a command in a positive way? Because it is the only way to train your dog to be obedient. The purpose of this rule is to keep you from the habit of letting frustration and anger rule your communication with your dog. You should find a way to work with your dog in an environment of love and trust. This does not mean you have to be a wimp or that you can never correct your dog. What it does mean is that you create a consistent lifestyle and your dog knows her place within your pack.

If you give your dog a command and something happens that prevents her from paying attention to you, then you still have to end that command in a positive way. How would you end that command in a positive way when you know your dog is not going to listen to you?

How do you end a command?

Yes, the answer is "All Done." Just tell your dog she is all done, then you can go on about your business and you can work on that command later. This rule is about realizing that there is no way your dog is going to do or complete the command you just gave. Now it is up to you to end it, and you cannot end it in a negative way, so All Done is your only option. All Done is not positive in the sense of how most people think of that word. All Done is a neutral way of ending the command in the moment of high distraction. By being neutral, you are being positive, not negative.

> **Rule Number Two:** Once you give a command, you cannot touch your dog or the leash, and you have to do everything in your power to get your dog to do that command.

There are two very important parts to this rule as well. First and foremost, you **cannot** touch your dog or her leash once you have given the command. The practice here is for you to learn how to make your dog want to do for you. What are you doing that either encourages or discourages your dog to make choices that you want? You get to see how you behave in situations where you now have no physical control over your dog.

In many of my podcasts, I give homework designed to get you to observe your dog in many situations in your home. How does your dog react when you do this? What does your dog do when you behave a certain way? This is the basis of **Rule Number Two**. Not just to observe your dog, but also to observe how you respond and react when your dog does something you don't want.

You cannot touch your dog or the leash once you have given the command **and** you have to do everything in your power to get your dog to do the command you just asked. Everything in your power! What do you have in your power to make your dog stop paying attention to whatever distractions there are and pay attention to you? You have only the three tools: Praise, Motivation, and Correction.

The purpose of this rule is to teach you to never give up on your dog. Knowing you only have the three tools and knowing that Praise is only to be used when your dog completes a command, you then realize you only have Motivation and Correction as tools to get your dog to pay attention to you.

By applying this rule, if you give a command to your dog and a distraction happens, you now know two things. One, that you must end the command in a positive way and two, that you cannot touch her or the leash. Let's go over the two tools, motivation and correction, you have to use to get your dog to pay attention to you in this distracting situation.

MOTIVATION

Remember, I said anything in your power. There are many things you can do to motivate your dog to pay attention to you during a distraction. Voice tone is a great motivator. Raise your voice, get excited, yell, whisper, and do whatever it takes to get your dog's attention. Body language is also an awesome motivator. Squat down, pat the ground, or jump up and down. Anything you need to do.

Don't give up. See if you can get your dog to change her focus and complete that command. Yes, treats and toys can be used. These are very high on the motivation scale and if you use them, I suggest you use them only once out of every 20 to 30 times you need to motivate your dog.

In the long run, you will be very happy with your dog's willingness to obey when you get her to make the choice or react the way you want her to without touching her or her leash. You will see better and better results because you will be making better and better decisions when telling your dog what you want from her. If some distractions are too much, work more often in low-distraction situations. If some things you use as motivation do not seem to work, look for things you do to which your dog pays attention.

Of course, remember that anything you overuse as a motivation creates and expectation from your dog. Knowing this, pay attention to what you use and mix it up. Find five or six things that work and use them sparingly.

CORRECTION

Sometimes at this point in training, I will ask a client, "Can you use correction?" It is about 50/50 on how people answer. The answer is yes. You can use correction; you just cannot touch your dog or her leash. You say "No." "No" means for your dog to stop doing what she is doing and pay attention to you. By now, in this stage of training, your dog should know what that word means.

With a good combination of correction and motivation, you should be able to get your dog's attention. Once you get her attention, it will be up to you get her to complete the command. Oh, and yes, you can repeat the command as often as you like. In the early stages of training, I tell owners to never repeat a command. By repeating a command, command becomes only motivation instead of a command. When you repeat a command consistently, your dog picks up on your voice tone, on your body language, and that you were not serious the first time you gave the command. Since you are now in a situation where you have to do everything in your power to complete the command you gave, it is okay to repeat it.

This rule is about never giving up on your dog when you know there is a possibility she will pay attention to you. Get her to complete the command, and you can proceed from there.

> **Rule Number Three:** If the command you gave is unsuccessful, before you do that command again, you have to pick up the leash and do that command at least 10 times before trying that command again without touching the leash (Stage 2) or off-leash (Stage 3).

Here is where my 10 to one ratio comes into play. If you have one unsuccessful event, then you have to practice ten times on the leash. When I ask an owner why, at this point the answer is almost always "So my dog gets the practice of doing that command." That is a wrong answer, because of what I told you at the beginning of this process. The rules are about you.

The practice is for you. You need to practice getting your dog to do the command willingly. When your dog is on the leash, and you are holding the leash, you have the opportunity to really practice what that command means. Are you being consistent? Are you being specific? Do you have to use any type of motivation or correction at this point (while on-leash) to get your dog to do the command you ask? This is a practice of awareness. Are you putting tension on the leash at any point? Are you giving the command only once? Are you giving the command and really expecting your dog to do that command?

In the past, I have covered the postulate that frustration and anger change your expectations. Here is where I really prove that theory. Most of the time, you are not aware that frustration has crept into your training. So how do you know? You have to pay attention to what you are doing at all times.

Tension on the leash is frustration. You don't believe your dog will do what you expect, so you guide her. Repeating a command is frustration. You don't think your dog is paying attention so you don't even give her a chance. Body language, such as moving in front of your dog or making a hand gesture so she can see it, is frustration. You don't think your dog will listen to you, so you change your positions or body language to make sure she sees you. In each of these scenarios, you let your frustrations change the expectations you have with your dog.

All this time, you thought the problem was with your dog. The problems are with you. If you are having an issue with a behavior, you need to adjust how you behave in order to get your dog to know and understand the rules. This works for every dog in every situation. When someone asks me what's the hardest breed of dog to train, I say, "The Human Breed."

So, why 10 times? Because when you break up that unsuccessful command with 10 successes, you have reached a point where you start to pay attention to how you communicate with your dog. Anything you do once or twice does not create, or get rid of, a habit. Anything you do over and over consistently creates a habit. If you see a behavior you don't like, it is because of how you react and respond to that behavior over and over again.

This ratio is very important throughout your training and is an easy way to keep up with your training on a daily basis. There is a video available through the website that goes along with Episode 050, "Correct Any Dog Behavior. Do This Five Minutes a Day," in the Discover Your Dog Podcasts. This video describes a way for you to create a calendar at your home to keep up with the work you are doing on any one behavior. The same can be used for training a basic command or just your daily routines. It all revolves around the 10 to one ratio.

SUCCESS

What do I mean by success? I mean perfect. You should have done the command perfectly for you to succeed in teaching your dog. Remember, these rules are about you and upon giving a command to your dog you should do nothing. If you dog responds to that command, it was done perfectly even if she hesitated or took a little extra time to do it. If you, the owner, use anything to motivate or correct your dog then you have created that the command was not perfect.

For Example, in a situation where you find that your dog is distracted, when use motivation or correction, then the command you just gave was not done perfectly. If you give the Come command and then when your dog hesitated, you said, "Aaargh, come!" then that command was not perfect. "Aaargh" was a correction, repeating the "come" was the motivation.

Rule Number Two is still in play here. If you have to use motivation or correction to get your dog to pay attention and make the right choice, do it. If you don't have to use those two tools, don't. You need to be aware of the level of distraction and the level of willingness from your dog.

The key to understanding whether or not you have had a successful command is whether or not you used motivation or correction. This can be very tricky. Sometimes you might bend over to get your dog's attention, which is motivation. Sometimes you may say a command, then move with your dog, which is also motivation. Sometimes you may give a command and then grunt to get your dog's attention, which is correction. Anything you use to motivate or correct has now made that command unsuccessful, and now you have to do that command 10 times on-leash.

In the same exact scenario from above, if you gave a command, your dog hesitated, you did nothing, and then your dog still completed the command? That would be perfect. This shows you how these rules have nothing to do with your dog. I cannot emphasize enough how you have to let your dog make the choice and react appropriately to that choice to really have good communication and an obedient dog.

IN CONCLUSION

Not all dogs are the same. They have many differing characteristics, personalities, and levels of willingness. This means you have to adapt. You have to be willing to take the time to find what works for your dog and continue to use what works and increase the willingness.

I work with many breeds of dog, and I see many levels of willingness from different breeds and even within the same breed. As an owner, you took on the responsibility to accept a living, loving creature into your life. It is up to you to live up to that responsibility.

By recognizing this willingness, you can adapt how you behave to get the best behavior from your dog. My dog, Oz, is an Australian Cattle Dog. He is a working breed and very loyal. It is very apparent in his demeanor and personality. Knowing this about his breed, I had an idea of what I was getting into before I adopted him. I was considering his willingness prior to making him a part of my family.

I was working with a client that has a Boston Terrier recently. She expressed some frustrations, and I said to her, "You have a breed that is very independent and is okay just being by himself sometimes." While I was saying this, she had dropped the leash, and her dog had gone off, found a toy, and started playing by himself. She was a great owner and did all the work to get her dog trained. The behaviors we saw at the beginning of training had taken a 180-degree turn and her dog was a joy to be around.

This training does not change your dog's personality. This training is to change the way you communicate so your dog understands your rules and boundaries and willingly abides by them. Will you still have issues? Yes; that is part of raising a family. The better you get to know your dog's personality, you will have the tools to encourage the best of that personality. The better the bond you create between you and your dog and the better fused your dog will be with your family. Your goal is that your dog knows the rules and is willing to do what you expect of her.

Enjoy Your Training and Be Impeccable with Your Dog.

Cheers,
Bennie

FDF RULES

- **The Ten to One Rule:**
  - For every *one* time you correct your dog for anything, you must praise your dog *10* times for doing the thing *you want* in that situation.
  - Until you have reached the ratio of 10:1 (praise: correction) in your dog's life for a specific action, she will always be willing to test that boundary. This could take a lifetime, so be patient and consistent.
- **The Rule of Praise:**
  - Praise must always be at a much higher level than the level of your correction.
  - The only time you are teaching your dog is when she is making a choice. You must use the correct tool at the time of the choice to get the results you want. Praise is the only way to truly teach your dog what you want in a way that makes her willing to do that thing.
- **The Rule of "No":**
  - Whenever you say "No," you must pull the leash. Whenever you pull the leash, you must say "No."
- **The Three Corrections Rule:**
  - Part 1: Frustration and anger change expectations. When working with your dog on a command she is learning, once you give three corrections for that command, reach down and put her into that position.
  - Part 2: The correction needs to get your dog to stop doing what she is doing and pay attention. This means

you need to correct to a level that gets her attention. If you correct out of anger, you are probably correcting too hard and chances are, you will not praise once your dog responds to what you asked. If you correct too softly, you are not making your dog stop doing what she is doing and pay attention. That would not be considered a correction.
- Part 3: If your dog knows a command and you still have to correct three times or more to get your dog to do that command, you are not using the tools properly. It is up to you to practice and increase your dog's willingness to do a certain command. You should only correct to the level you need to get your dog's attention, and you should practice praising for doing that command more often. Motivation can be used, but you need to be aware if your dog starts to expect that motivation.
- **The Rules of Distraction:**
  - Your dog must do any *one* thing *10* times in a row before moving up to the next level of training.
  - Whenever you use something as a distraction during a training session, after the session is done, you have to assess whether or not your dog should participate with that item.
  - If you use something as a distraction and your dog breaks the command three times with it, then that distraction is too much and you need to lower the threshold.
- **Always** choose motivation over correction when there is a choice. When you are using motivation as a tool, your dog is more likely to remember the command and more likely to want to do that command.
- **"All Done"** means your dog is finished with the last command you gave. Use this command throughout your

workout. Usually the novice trainer will only use this command at the end of the entire workout or while praising for completing a command. This causes your dog to think she is done with the workout entirely and/or that praise is also a release.
- **Stay** is incorporated in all commands and does not need to be said. Your dog is released when you say "All Done."
- **Always** end a command or a training session on a positive note.
- **Enjoy** the workouts so your dog will enjoy you.
- **The Three Stages for Off-Leash Training:**
    o **Stage 1 – On-Leash:** This is a two to three-month process and everything is done on-leash.
    o **Stage 2 – Not Touching Leash:** This is a four to five-month process where you will start the Three Rules of Consistency. You will be asking your dog to do commands while still on the leash, and you cannot touch your dog or the leash once you have given a command.
    o **Stage 3 – Off-Leash:** This is a six to seven-month process and you will now start asking your dog to do commands with no leash at all.
- **The 3 Rules of Consistency:**
    o Whenever you give a command, no matter what happens, you always have to end it in a positive way.
    o Once you give a command, you cannot touch your dog or the leash, and you have to do everything in your power to get your dog to do that command.
    o If the command you gave is unsuccessful, before you can do that command again, you have to pick up the leash and do that command at least 10 times before trying that command again without touching the leash (Stage 2) or off-leash (Stage 3).

FDF DEFINITIONS

- **Obedience:** The willingness to obey.
- **Praise:** Any attention for a behavior when your dog has made a choice. In order to teach your dog, you must give positive attention when she has made the choice you want her to make. This is the *only* way you are teaching and training your dog to be obedient.
- **Motivation:** Anything *positive* you use to get your dog to pay attention to you, and then make a choice. Anything that is overused as a motivation creates an expectation from your dog.
- **Correction:** Anything *negative* you use to make your dog stop doing what she is doing and pay attention to you. Anything that is overused as a correction creates fear in your dog.
- **Heel:** Walk at your left side and sit when you stop.
- **Come:** Come to you and sit.
- **Sit:** Put your butt to the ground.
- **Down:** Lie down, all the way on the ground.
- **Place:** Go to a mat and lie down on, or touch, the mat.
- **No:** Stop what you are doing and pay attention to me.
- **All-Done:** Your dog is finished with the last command you gave.

FDF POSTULATES

Below I have written out each postulate. I also have brief discussion points about each. The discussion points are for you to think further as to how each postulate can relate to your specific issue.

Each description will give you a little insight as to why I believe each theory to be true. I also hope to explain how each postulate pertains to you and to the dog you wish to fuse with your family.

- **Praise is the only way you are truly teaching your dog. It is the only way you are going to get your dog to be willing to do what you want.**

Praise is the only way you truly **teach** your dog. Most people never learn this concept because motivation and correction also seem to be ways to teach. When we look at these tools in human terms, it makes a lot of sense. This is why the above statement is so confusing; As humans, you want to analyze each of the tools and determine why to use that tool. This is an issue when training people, they always want to know why. If you see even the smallest result from either of the tools, you think it is what works with your dog every time.

To compare a dog's reactive behavior to the human's analytical behavior does not work in the learning and teaching process. Why? Because at some point, the human is going to make a change in their thought process which will change how they behave in any given situation. Once a dog learns to act a certain way, in any given situation, they will act the same way until trained or taught otherwise. Let's go through some examples.

If you were a child growing up during the Cold War you were likely taught that "The Russians" are evil and want to destroy "The Americans." All your life, you were bombarded with this information to the point that you believe it is true. One day in your travels for work, you are stuck at an airport and go to the bar. Only one seat is available, and you sit next to a gentleman you have never met. You strike up a conversation and because you both are stuck there for hours, you talk and find you have many things in common. Your family, friends, and ideologies are very similar. You even like the same drinks and food. After talking and getting to know this gentleman, you notice a slight accent and ask him, "Where are you from? I notice a slight accent in your voice." He tells you, "Russia."

Now you have to analyze your new friend, what you have been taught all your life, and decide how you are going to behave now. You have so many choices. You now get to decide whether or not to continue with your old beliefs and terminate your conversation, or you can change how you behave and continue talking and getting to know this great person you just met.

Dogs cannot and will not ever be able to analyze to this extent. They can only take what they have learned and make decisions based on these lessons.

My Oz was rescued from being put down because of his aggression toward other dogs. He was very possessive and protective of his owner at the time. When I met Oz, I could see how all of this behavior was being reinforced by the current foster care person. I decided to take him into our kennel, train him, and work on introducing him to other dogs so that he might be adoptable in the future.

He lived at the kennel for a year. During that time, he had many dog friends, he was allowed to roam around the house, and he played in many of the groups. He was given freedoms many of the other dogs weren't given, because we really wanted to concentrate on how he behaved in social situations and to reinforce his good behavior. He is now so good with a dog he accepts, that the other dog can get away with just about anything around him. He will let a child, another dog, or an adult take anything from his mouth. I have seen a 4-year-old pull a bone from his mouth. Oz looked up at me because he knew he was going to get praised for that behavior. He will even let another dog push him away from his food bowl, while eating, and just sit back. Why? Because this is what he was taught to do. With consistent reinforcement, he thinks this is the only way to behave. There is no changing this behavior unless he feels threatened or motivated to change his reactions.

Notice, I said unless he feels threatened or motivated to change his reactions. This is where I started realizing what motivation and correction really were. They are tools to start the process of changing behaviors for a dog, not tools to teach. The only tool to teach is praise. When the choice is made and the reaction from you, the owner, is praising and pleasing, then you are teaching your dog to behave and react that way. The better you are at recognizing that a choice has been made, and being consistent with your positive response, the quicker you will teach. That choice being made will happen with more frequency and consistency, as well.

Discussion Points:
1) Understanding the difference between reactive and analytical behavior is important. This is why the examples of teaching children sound great, but the result is that you think your dog is making decisions based on the same analytical skills.
2) Understand the importance of consistent awareness and reactions to good behavior from your dog.

- **When you have reached a lifetime ratio of praising your dog 10 times more than you have ever corrected, your dog will always choose to do the behavior you want, even if you are not there.**

A lifetime ratio of 10 to one! This means you have praised your dog 10 more times for doing what you want her to do than you have ever corrected her for doing what you don't want.

I read a science report once about the human brain. In this report, it said that certain thoughts that we have over and over again start to create a path in the brain, and this is why we have habits, bad or good. It went on to say that once those paths are formed, it is very difficult to vary from them. It takes effort, time, consistency, and conscious awareness to step off that path and form a new one.

I pictured riding my bike through the woods. The path is cleared and easy, and I am not going to stray from it without getting hurt or lost. If, at some point, I want to create a new path or shortcut, I may have to start by getting off my bike and walking through the brush to know where to start. Then I would start clearing the path, maybe using some tools or just walking that path again and again.

See where I am going with this metaphor? It takes effort, time, consistency, and conscious awareness to start that new path. The new path you are on is thinking (or speaking) in the affirmative. You have to be consciously aware of what choices your dog is making, use the tools you are learning here, and start to create that path to better behavior.

In my podcasts and training sessions, I talk about this new awareness like this: "At first you will unconsciously react to your dog 100 times before you catch yourself and make the change. The next time you may catch yourself after 50 times of unconscious reactions. The next time it will take 25 times, then 10 times, then every five times, then even every other time you will catch yourself." This is forming that new habit of looking for your dog to behave in a certain way, instead of reacting to the behaviors you don't want.

The problem becomes making up for all of those unconscious reactions that reinforced the bad behavior in the first place. The goal is to understand your consistencies, inconsistencies, and improve your communication. Most people will not reach the lifetime ratio of 10 times more praises than corrections in the life of their dog. But, with that purpose in mind, you will change your focus and begin the process of praising more than you ever correct.

Here is why this is a postulate. I realized I had reached that ratio with my Molly in two areas of her life: going potty outside and choosing to stay on the floor. She would rather go potty outside than inside. When I would see her potty outside on occasion, I still praised her, even as an adult. As she got older, she had more accidents, but they were only during the night when I was asleep or if I had been gone for long periods of time. Usually, those accidents were located near the door leading outside.

The other behavior, staying on the floor, she did even when I was not at home. She had free reign of my house when I was gone, and she had places to sleep all over the house. Those places were where I would usually find her when I came home. Now with Oz,

I have not yet reached a lifetime of praising him for staying on the floor over choosing to get on the furniture.

Discussion Points:
1) Knowing what you want, learning how to make your dog make the choices, then being aware when your dog makes the choices you want are keys to reaching a lifetime ratio of 10 to one.
2) This takes a long time. If you don't know the history of an adopted or adult dog, then you don't know how many times a bad behavior may have been reinforced in its lifetime.

- **Structure means rules! By creating and abiding by these rules, you will always be doing the same things and always expecting the same results.**

This is the basic theory upon which my entire training is based. What is life without rules? In human life, we call these laws. These laws are not to be confused with the laws of government; I'm discussing the laws of the universe, although both can be applied in this discussion. One such law is the law of gravity. I am not scientific, and I am not going into the basics of this law, but you must understand this law cannot be broken. In other words, if you jump off a building, you are only going one way, because of the law of gravity.

When you accept a dog into your home as a part of your family, you create structure. This structure is created no matter your intentions. Problems start to arise when you accept different results concerning any one behavior. Think about the structure in your home. Is it consistent? Most people would say yes to this question because they do things on auto-pilot and lack awareness. Awareness of inconsistencies is the key to fixing the behavior problem.

When I do a primary consultation with an owner, most of the time, the owner begins to see the things they do that encourage, rather than correct, a problem behavior. If they recognize this early, many times I get the comment, "You are not training my dog, are you? You are really training me." This is truly the case in every situation, in every consultation, in every evaluation, and with every behavior modification I do.

Discussion Points:
1) Potty Training. Where do you want your dog to go to the bathroom? Do you consistently take her to that spot?
2) Jumping up. Why does your dog keep jumping up? Are you consistent about making her stay on all fours?

- **Dogs are reactive. Good choices or bad choices become reinforced for the attention you give in the moment of the choice (or reaction) from your dog. Dogs do not analyze. Because of this, your dog does not make choices based on situational analysis.**

Praise works as a teaching method because you give praise during the moment of a choice (or reaction) that you want. For example, if your dog chooses to stay on all four paws when greeting a person and you respond in a pleasing, praising way, you will be teaching your dog to continue this behavior. This is an example of how you are supposed to use praise.

Giving attention for a behavior you don't want is also teaching, and can be considered using the tool of praise. For example, if your dog greets a person by jumping on them and you yell at her, grab her, and hold her down angrily, you are giving attention to that behavior. Even though you yelled at her or said "No" during the time of the jump, it is still attention and still reinforces that behavior. This is an example of how we use praise (attention) to reinforce a behavior we don't want.

Giving positive attention to a choice or reaction you don't want is very common as well. For example, say your dog is going to greet someone coming into your house and the person slams the door behind them. Your dog reacts by running off, tail tucked, then quickly returning and giving a low growl toward that person. You reach down and stroke your dog telling her it is okay and try to coax her toward that person while using pleasing and calming tones. At this moment, you are now giving positive attention toward a behavior you don't want, growling and fear. This is an example of reinforcing, or teaching through praise, a behavior you don't want.

Furthermore, dogs are not analytical. Your dog will never make a choice based on analyzing the situation. For example, your dog jumps up on your friend and then you scold her in the moment. An hour later, you find that your dog peed in another room when you were not paying attention. Most people would call this action from the dog spiteful. To be spiteful, your dog has to have analyzed the situation and done that behavior because of how you reacted when she jumped up. This is not possible. It is possible for your dog to believe you are lower in the hierarchy. Or, your dog has learned to go in a place where you are not watching and when you are not paying attention. If these examples are true for you, there are many actions and reactions your dog may make with regards to how she would treat you, but to have analytical thoughts and behave accordingly is not how a dog's brain works.

Discussion Points:
1) Praise can be (and is often) used to teach both behaviors you want and behaviors you don't want.
2) Dogs cannot be jealous, envious, spiteful, or any other emotion that requires analytical thought. Because of this, you have to react to your dog's choices and reactions in order to teach what you want from your dog.

- **Anything you do once or twice does not create a behavior or correct a behavior. The quicker you catch yourself and correct yourself, the quicker you and your dog will learn.**

To go along with the previous postulate, praise is the only way you are truly teaching your dog. Recognizing and praising once or twice will not teach your dog to behave a certain way. As an owner, you have to be consistent. Even if you are being very consistent about how you use the tools Praise, Motivation, and Correction, if others around you are not being consistent, your dog is getting mixed signals and will continue to test the boundaries.

I love going into a home and hearing an owner say, "My dog was potty trained in three days." I hear this a lot. Usually if that owner becomes a client, I get the stories of how the dog is having accidents or was hiding to go to the bathroom in the house without the owner realizing it for a long time. Many people think they can do something once or twice with their dog, get the results they expected, and have it stick.

When I go into a home for the first time, I give an example of how I taught Molly to choose to stay on the floor. In my example, it took two corrections as she chose to get on the couch. The third time I put her into that situation, she chose to stay on the floor, and I praised her for making that decision. Then I say, "This is when most people quit!" It is true. When you are working with your dog and she makes one or two good choices, you think she has learned that thing, and you stop working on it. This is the beginning of your inconsistency and why you end up having to correct your dog a few days later for that behavior. It is also why you get so frustrated and wonder why you can't get your dog to "stop" doing something.

As a rule, when I show an owner how to work on a certain behavior, I suggest working on that *one* thing 10 times a day. That's it. The goal is to get at least one praise when setting your dog up in these situations. Start with temptations that your dog will resist easily. The better your dog gets, the bigger the distractions you can introduce.

Discussion Points:
1) The length of time it takes your dog to learn something and make the choices you want depends on how consistent you are and how aware you are about giving your dog attention during the choices.
2) This is why the **Ten to One Rule** applies and is so important.

- **Touch is the biggest reward you can give your dog. Any time you touch your dog, you are rewarding whatever behavior your dog is doing at that time.**

Teaching that touch is only a form of praise is a tough one, because you touch your dog in so many situations. Not only that, but most trainers, veterinarians, groomers, and other professionals in the dog world will use touch as a correction in certain situations, and it works for them. It works because they are dog professionals and know how to apply the touch appropriately to get the results they need. Teaching you the correct way to touch your dog so that it is a correction is a tedious and unnecessary process, because it will be done ineffectively for the most part. Also touch, as a form of correction, comes very close to crossing the line of abuse, if done incorrectly.

This is why I teach to avoid touching your dog, in any way, during a choice or a reaction. It is also a great way to create awareness on your part. If you are giving attention for a behavior, then you are praising your dog. Even if the attention is negative, it is still attention. This includes spanking your dog, holding your dog down, pushing your dog away, picking your dog up, shaking your dog, or kneeing your dog. These are the negative ways you touch your dog while thinking you are correcting a behavior. Those are also common ways that many dog professionals tell you to react to your dog in certain situations.

When you avoid touching your dog in situations of correction, you create awareness in two ways. One, you are now looking at other ways to make your dog stop doing a behavior you don't want. Two, you are looking for positive praise opportunities to teach your dog what you want by touching her to praise her.

Discussion Points:
1) Know why it is a reinforcement of behavior when you touch your dog and not a correction.
2) Understand that the concept has to do only with you, because you are not a professional in this industry.

- **Motivation is anything positive you use to create a situation where your dog pays attention to you, then makes a choice. Anything overused as a motivation creates an expectation from your dog.**

Notice the difference between motivation and praise. Motivation is something *positive,* whereas praise is just attention and can be negative, positive, or neutral. The other big difference is that motivation is used to make your dog pay attention, then make a choice. Once your dog makes the choice, any attention you give at that moment becomes praise.

The key is the choice--that you made your dog make a choice, or that your dog made a choice on her own. The key is your response in regards to the choice. To get your dog in a situation, then encourage her to behave how you want her to in that situation is motivation.

There are many ways you can motivate. The obvious motivations are treats, toys, and noises such as clicks or whistles. The not-so-obvious motivations are your dog's name, body language, such as a wave of your arms, and subtle voice tones such as a high-pitched, cheerful tone or a calming tone. You have used one or all of those motivations at one time or another.

The problem with using motivation as a method of training is that anything you overuse as motivation creates expectations from your dog. If your dog expects something from you in order to do something for you, is that really a willingness to obey? This is why I teach that motivation is a good tool, but not a good method of training.

Most motivation-based trainers will tell you that it is best to use motivation to get your dog to learn a behavior or command, then slowly remove that motivation when working on the behavior or command. To me, this is like saying the best way to stop smoking is to continue smoking and reduce the number of cigarettes you smoke by one a week until you are not smoking any more. This may work for some, but it does not work for everyone. The same goes for your dog. Reducing the motivation might work, but your goal should be to create obedience (the willingness to obey) from the beginning, not work toward obedience later.

Discussion Points:
1) Knowing the difference between praise and motivation is in the definitions. The key to understanding the difference is knowing whether a choice is being made or if the dog expects something from you.
2) Being aware when and where you are using both obvious and subtle forms of motivation is very important to understand if you are using motivation as a method or just a tool when training.

- **Correction is anything negative you use to make your dog stop doing what she is doing and pay attention to you. Anything overused as a correction creates fear in your dog.**

I have been asked if it is possible to negatively motivate my dog. The answer is no; negative motivation would be better defined as correction. Correction is anything negative you do to get your dog to stop doing what she is doing and pay attention. Therefore, if you use something that creates fear or a desire to *not* do a behavior, then you are correcting, as long as your dog stops doing what she is doing and pays attention.

When there is a behavior you never want from your dog, or a behavior you want your dog to stop doing, that is what you correct for. The purpose of a correction is not to create the fear; *the purpose of a correction is to get your dog to learn there is a choice in any given situation.* This means that you have to be ready to get your dog to make another choice once a correction has been used. It does not mean you have to get her to make the choice right then; it means you have to be aware that you corrected. In order for you to teach your dog how to behave in that situation, you have to get her to make the right choice 10 more times than she made the wrong choice. If you don't know what you expect your dog to do, then you will only be overusing the correction tool, and you will create fear.

There are two big issues I have with correction as a method of training. One, I never want my dog to fear me. I don't want her to be afraid for doing something I don't want. I don't want my dog to fear something I expect her to do. Stated in the affirmative: I want my dog to love and trust me, I want my dog to want to understand what I expect her not to do, and I want my dog to do what I expect her to do willingly.

The second issue I have is that overuse creates fear. Dogs, just like humans, are very willing to test the boundaries of fear. At some point, your dog will test you in a situation when you have used, or overused, fear because you have never taught your dog there was another choice. If your dog does not know there is another choice and faces that situation over and over again, eventually she will test the boundaries to see if you are going to stay consistent.

This is where I started understanding how people think a dog can turn on an owner later in life. It's not that the dog turned on the owner. It's that the owner never gave the dog another choice to make and continued using the corrective method to "teach" their dog. The dog will eventually get more aggressive because of the innate willingness to test the boundaries.

Discussion Points:
1) Corrections are negative. If you do something in a positive way to "correct" your dog, then it is motivation, not correction.
2) Using correction as a method of training has only the purpose of making the dog *stop* a behavior. Using this tool as a method never allows the dog to learn, or understand, that there is a choice.

- **To understand what you want is most important. When you put behavior into terms of what you *don't want*, that behavior is the only thing that gets attention. Attention for a behavior reinforces that behavior, whether it is good or bad attention.**

We call this "Thinking or Speaking in the Affirmative." Whenever you want your dog to do a certain behavior, you have to know what behavior you want, state that behavior affirmatively, and then look for that behavior to happen. The only way you will ever be able to praise your dog for that affirmative behavior is if you are looking for it to happen. Most of you only react to the negative behavior, or the behavior you *don't* want.

If you only state things in the negative, like "I **don't** want my dog to jump up," you will then only look for and react to that behavior. In this case you, the owner, are only looking for and reacting to the *jumping up* behavior.

For every behavior you state as what *don't* want, as what you want to *stop*, as what you want your dog to *quit doing*, or as what you need your dog to do *without*; there is an affirmative, alternate behavior. You need to find and look for the affirmative behavior, or you will only give attention to the negative behavior and cause it to continue.

Stating what you don't want is ingrained in you. This, again, is a practice in awareness. The practice for me comes in every aspect of my life. Instead of asking my friend, "Don't forget we have a meeting on Thursday." I now state, "Remember we have a meeting this Thursday." By practicing in my everyday life, I can see how many times I state things negatively. I also see how often others in my life talk that way. There are only a couple people that know what I am doing when I restate their negative statements, and we will always laugh about it. I do not correct anyone else; the practice for me is noticing.

If you have been listening to the Discover Your Dog Podcast, you will hear many occasions where my co-host and I correct each other or work on talking in the affirmative with each other. Even then, it is sometimes difficult and we fall back to the negative comments. I have learned if you can state something in the negative, there is always a way to state it in the affirmative.

When you see what behaviors you want from your dog, you have the opportunity and power to reinforce that good behavior through positive praise. Why? Because you now have the power to look for an option. Remember, praise is attention for any behavior at that moment. If you give attention (any attention) to the negative behavior, the negative behavior continues to happen. If you give attention (positive attention) to the affirmative behavior, that behavior continues to happen.

Discussion Points:
1) Creating the awareness of stating behaviors in the affirmative takes practice. Why does it come so naturally for us humans to state things in the negative?
2) Make a list of behaviors you don't want, then make an alternate list of how each of those behaviors can be stated in the affirmative.

- **Consistency is the key to training your dog. You must know how you want your dog to behave, then act consistently in every given situation.**

Yes, you all know what it means to be consistent. The problems come when you don't realize you are not being consistent. This takes awareness, and awareness comes through practice. Once you are aware of how you are communicating, then you can change it. If you are not aware, you cannot change.

So many times I ask an owner to tell their dog to sit. The owner, who has told me their dog knows this command, will say the command to the dog, and the dog will not react. Before the owner even realizes it, usually after I have pointed it out, they have repeated the command many times. If I ask them later to tell me how many times they said the command before the dog did the sit, they rarely are able to answer correctly because they were not aware. The habit of repeating the command multiple times has become so ingrained that when it happens, it seems natural.

Once I point this out, you would think an owner would get it and never repeat the command again, right? No. Sometimes I have to point it out many times over the course of months for the awareness to set in. Even then, when I am no longer doing the training, old habits will creep back in and the repetitions begin. This is why it is so difficult to be consistent; you are only vaguely aware of when you are not being consistent. If you have no awareness at all, the habit will never change.

Is it wrong to repeat a command? No, but the point of any method or tool of training is that you have to know what you are communicating in every given situation. To say a command once, such as sit, and expect it to be done is what you, as a trainer, should always expect. Once you repeat the command, it is no longer a command. It now becomes motivation.

From our rules, you know that anything overused as a motivation creates an expectation. If you repeat a command, typically you will raise your voice or follow the repetition with body language. Once you do either of these things, your dog will begin to expect you to do these things every time. Your dog will wait until you reach a certain tone with the command or use certain body language prior to doing that command.

Being aware of this is very difficult. If you start to become aware when you are repeating the command, you then have to change how you respond to your dog. This is where the practice comes in. If you are not practicing how you communicate to your dog with intention, you will never be able to break the habit of miscommunication. With practice, you start to recognize your inconsistencies more often. The more you practice, the quicker you realize what you're doing and the more consistent you become.

Discussion Points:
1) How do body language and voice tone play a part in inconsistent behavior from you, the owner?
2) What other inconsistencies happen that you, the owner, may not be aware of?

- **The energy or emotions you emit when working, playing, or just hanging out with your dog will radiate to your dog. Your dog will mimic this energy depending on the situation and level of connection you have with your dog. Think of your leash as a conductor of whatever energy you are feeling at that time.**

This postulate focuses on the bond you have with your dog. The stronger that bond, the more you will see how your energy and emotions will affect your dog's behavior and mood. Even a person that does not have a great bond with their dog will see mood changes from a dog when they have high mood swings as well.

The better your communication the more you will see how your dog does reflect your energy at every level. You will also notice when your dog may be feeling bad or having a highly energetic day as well. The reason for this is that you are learning to recognize signs, body language, and general consistencies with your dog.

I would compare it to a mother of a very young child that has not learned to form words yet. When a baby makes certain sounds and facial expressions, a mother knows exactly what their child wants. As you develop your skill of looking for what you want from your dog, you will start to recognize and know what your dog's needs are as well.

Discussion Points:
1) Have you ever noticed that when you feel a certain way your dog acts differently depending on your mood?
2) Is it possible to have a high-level energy connection with a dog?

- **Dominance is about trust. If your dog trusts you will be consistent, she is less likely to test the boundaries. When you create trust, you create great communication and an incredible bond between you and your dog.**

In the dog world, the highest participant in the pack is the one that is the most consistent and trusted. Dogs look to other dogs and humans to be protectors and faithful pack members. Dogs are also much more consistent than humans. This is why I tell many owners that dog is dog's best friend, not man's best friend. Dogs understand each other much better than they understand us. As dogs become more and more domesticated, I see even the dog's communications are starting to grow further apart from each other.

It is important to learn to react to your dog's behavior in appropriate ways in order to get your dog to understand what you want from them or how you expect them to behave. The typical issues dog owners fall into are reacting only to bad behaviors, usually inappropriately. This creates mistrust from your dog, mainly because you react to the bad behaviors differently every time. You may yell, you may "knee" your dog, you may push your dog into a command (sit or down), or you may stroke or try to calm your dog down. All of these different reactions are things you are doing to correct the behavior, and they are very different reactions for the same situations.

Another example is how you use commands in so many different situations. It is confusing for your dog. The best example is the "Come" command. "Come" should mean one specific thing. In the Discover Your Dog Podcast Episode 002, Specificity, we talk about the importance of understanding the purpose of the basic commands. "Come" is used in so many inconsistent ways that it is difficult for you dog to grasp this command. "Come" to come inside, "Come" to go outside, "Come" to go for a ride, "Come" to eat, "Come" to play, etc., etc. There are so many ways you use that word (even though you think you are giving a command), in so many situations, that the word "come" becomes confusing to your dog.

Performing different actions in the same situations is very confusing for your dog. If your dog is seemingly being defiant or stubborn in situations you thought you were being consistent, the truth is that you aren't, or there is some other inconsistency going on in your life. This is why your dog behaves in a defiant or stubborn way.

The more consistent your actions are, the more your dog will trust that you are going to act in a certain way, and the more likely it is that you will take the dominant role and your dog will stop testing the boundaries of the hierarchy. Most dogs want this structure. They want you to take the role as the dominant and they want to trust you. When you take this role, they get to be a dog. I say most because a very small percentage of dogs are truly dominant dogs. They do not make good pets.

Discussion Points:
1) Understand how dogs react to families that are incongruent with training beliefs or styles.
2) Understand how owners create mistrust through inconsistent actions with any one behavior from their dog.

- **Dog is dog's best friend! Dogs understand each other much better than they understand humans.**

When you think about body language and voice tone being the main way a dog learns from us, it makes sense that a dog would pick up on these simple cues from another dog much easier. This is why I believe this postulate to be true.

It is not that humans cannot have a close connection with their dog, but because how we process thoughts is so different, there is a huge disconnect. Because humans are analytical thinkers, the tendency is to think dogs are the same. Many humans feel dogs are analytical thinkers as well. This type thinking creates many problems with communication between you and your dog.

As dogs are reactive thinkers, it would make sense that they would best understand another reactive thinker. This does not mean that dogs have perfect communication. What it does mean is that in most social situations, dogs will relate to another dog quicker and sometime form a better bond than they can with a human. This is especially true if the human has weak communication skills with their dog.

Discussion Points:
1) What type of body language do you think dogs pick up on the fastest?
2) Are there certain things you can do, especially when it comes to body language, that will help your dog understand you better?

- Making your dog do an obedience command while working on a behavior does not result in the dog understanding what you want in a given situation. It teaches your dog to do that command with bigger distractions.

Giving your dog a command does not fix a behavior. As we discussed in all of the commands, doing commands is just a way to get your dog focused, teach you to be consistent, teach your dog where she belongs in the hierarchy, and give her self-confidence. The commands will not fix any specific behavior.

By learning to teach the commands, you should also be learning how to teach your dog in any given situation. You have to look for the behavior you want, see that your dog made that choice or reaction, and praise in a timely manner. I will give the example of teaching your dog to drop something on command.

Example: There may be a time when you want your dog to drop something she has in her mouth, such as food that could make her sick, an article of your clothing, or just a ball you'd like to throw again. In any of these cases, it would be a great behavior if she would drop the item on command.

When I teach this command to a client, I use the phrase "Drop it." For this example's sake, that is the phrase I will use, though you can use anything you want, such as "give it," "let go, or just "drop."

The first and most common mistake you will do is go for the item once your dog has dropped it. This creates a game for the dog and gets her attention from you. Your dog will drop the item, and then immediately go for it again. Or, she will wait for you to go for it before diving at the item, then taking off or holding on to it. This is part of the game for your dog, and it tends to get her a lot of attention. If your dog dives for the ball, most likely you will grab your dog or yell at her to give it back. By giving your dog this attention, you are teaching her that this is how you expect her to behave. The game gets bigger and bigger and it becomes more difficult for you to get things from your dog. Your dog may start to steal things with the intent of getting attention, even if it is negative attention.

In this example, the goal is to get your dog to choose to do what you want her to do, then praise her for that choice. You want her to drop the ball on command. First, give the command, "Drop it." When she drops the ball, you should be praising her, not going for the ball. Pet her while talking to her in an excited voice, and push her away from the ball. The goal is to get her to pay attention to you while you are praising her, and draw her attention away from the ball. While you are holding her away from the ball, reach back, get the ball, then throw it for her again. When she brings it back again, say "Drop it" however many times you need to until she drops it. Go through the same process above. Now you are giving your dog attention for the behavior you want her to do, and she will be more and more likely to drop the item the more you are praising her for that choice.

Above is a basic example, and there are many other scenarios that could play a part in teaching your dog to drop an item. For further explanation of this specific behavior, listen to the Discover Your Dog Podcast. There are many other issues you may encounter with this command, such as running away with the item, getting an item that could potentially hurt your dog, and holding on to the item for a long time.

The reason I went through that example was to show you how giving your dog a basic command is not going to help you in the situation above. You could make your dog sit, and then she is just sitting. If she dropped the item while in the sit command and you praised her, you would be only praising her for sitting, not dropping the ball.

When teaching the commands and working on behavior, it is important to know what you want your dog to do. In the above example, you would be reacting to just that, dropping the ball.

Discussion Points:
1) When working on specific behaviors, it is important to know the purpose in teaching the commands and why it is not necessary to use the commands.
2) When learning to teach basic commands, what are you ultimately learning to do in every given situation?

- **The Sit command is just getting your dog to sit. It is not about focus or correction, although the Sit command is used for these two reasons more often than any other command.**

Sit is just sit. That is it! The most common mistake that people make with the Sit command is to use it as a correction or to stop a behavior. The problem with that is once you release your dog from the command, how will she behave then?

Sit is not a fix. The Sit command will not stop your dog from doing the behavior you want to correct. At best, you may get your dog to refocus on you, and then it is up to you to make sure your dog makes the choice you want. Even if your dog does sit in a very distracting situation, all you are doing is getting your dog to do a command with more distraction. This may seem appropriate at the time, but it does not help the end result of any behaviors you may be working on at that time.

The best use of the Sit command is for you to practice looking for praise opportunities. When you teach this command, your practice should be saying the command only once, then expecting your dog to do it. Knowing when your dog is ready to do the Sit command on her own, then watching for those praise opportunities is practicing awareness. You are being aware of getting what you want from your dog and praising her for that, instead of reacting to only the bad behaviors you don't want.

Discussion Points:
1) What purpose does the Sit command serve?
2) In what everyday situation would it be proper and necessary to use the Sit command?

- **Your voice tone is a main way your dog learns from you. A dog can pick up subtle changes in your voice and will respond according to your level of sincerity. Coupled with body language, these are the two most important communication tools you use when communicating with your dog.**

One thing I hear a lot when training is for an owner to repeat a command. Many times, this repetition is more than three to four times before a dog reacts, if she ever does. During the repetition of the command the owner changes the tone of the command. This tone change, no matter how subtle, is noted by the dog. The dog will soon learn when you are serious by listening for that certain tone.

Voice tone and body language work together. Your dog can note a serious tone and recognize that you are not really that serious by your body language. When you are getting frustrated with your dog take a personal inventory of the tones you are using and the body language you are projecting. You may learn why your dog turns away from you or "just doesn't listen." The fact is your dog hears you; she knows to wait for you to be serious before reacting.

I compare it to counting for a child. Most parents count to three. If the child hears a parent counting they usually don't even react until the parent reaches three. I have known parents to put a two-and-a-half into the count just because they think the child is not hearing them. Usually the count gets louder and louder just as you might do when repeating a command to your dog.

Another thing about body language and voice tone is that they work very well together when training a dog. This is why you learn hand signs when training. Because a dog understands body language so well, it makes sense to use signs as well as verbal cues when training basic commands.

Discussion Points:
1) Do you have a certain number of times you will repeat a command before making your dog do that thing?
2) What signs do you use in everyday situations when communicating with your dog?

- **The Heel command is about focus for your dog. This is the command used to warm up, get ready to work, and start the workout. Heel is rarely used in everyday situations.**

The Heel command is the most misunderstood command in dog training. Most people think that the Heel command is to be used all the time in walks and social situations. "Heel" means your dog walks at your left side and sits when you stop. That is it. For your dog, this means she cannot sniff around, she cannot take a pee break, and she cannot be on your right side. Also, when you stop, your dog has to sit. Sit is incorporated into the Heel command, and once your dog is in the sit, she cannot get up until you give another command or release her from the Heel command.

Heel is not meant for normal everyday walks, and for the most part (or at least I think it should be this way), you will never use the Heel command as a part of your daily routine once the training sessions are over. It is too structured and rigid to keep your dog in a Heel command in normal, everyday situations.

Another way many people use the Heel command is to make their dog come. Again, this not only confuses the Come command, which is already confusing enough, it also now confuses the Heel command. It is important to understand what you are asking your dog to do when you give the Heel command. Stay specific to the purpose of the command.

The Heel command is to get your dog focused and ready to work. It is the first thing taught in most training situations for that reason. When used appropriately, the Heel command is what you use to get your dog into workouts and to focus on whatever is new for that day. It should only be done during the one to three workout sessions you will be doing for that day. The Heel command is one command that is rarely, if ever, used once the basic training is over. The Heel command has little use in everyday situations. If you are using the Heel command outside of training, you are likely using it wrong and not being clear to your dog.

Discussion Points:
1) Heel is the most misunderstood command. Name two ways most people misuse the Heel command.
2) What does heel mean and what is the purpose of the Heel command?

- **The Come command is about focus for you, the owner. Teaching the Come command has nothing to do with your dog. It has to do with your understanding of what it means to be specific and consistent.**

The Come command has nothing to do with your dog, as far as I am concerned. The Come command is the most misused and confusing command in training. It is confusing because of all the ways you use the command to get your dog's attention. "Come" to come inside, "Come" to go outside, "Come" to eat, "Come" to go for a walk, or "Come" to go for a ride.

When you use the Come command in so many generic ways, it really has no meaning. When you say "Come," you should mean only one thing: "Come to me and sit." Yet, many people don't mean anything except "Pay attention." To avoid this confusion and misuse, you have to be very aware of when you are saying the Come command to your dog. What did you want when you said the word "Come," and did it have the same meaning as when you said it last?

The Come command has nothing to do with your dog because the Come command is the best command when it comes to teaching **you** to be aware of what you are saying to your dog. It is also great for learning to be specific with all of your commands. Anytime you say the word "Come" to your dog, you should mean and expect only one thing. You should expect your dog to come to you and sit. This means that when you say the command, you stay put until your dog completes the Come command by sitting near you. You cannot walk away, and you cannot start the big praise until your dog is sitting. Doing this one thing with this one command, Come, is a huge practice in awareness and specificity.

Until you can master saying one word to mean so much, you will also struggle with other commands.

Discussion Points:
1) Why is the Come command the most misused and confusing command?
2) What two things are best learned from using the Come command appropriately?

- **The Down command is *the* most important command you will teach your dog. This is the command where your dog will take its place in your pack, depending on how *willing* she is to do this command.**

Down means for your dog to lay down all the way. My personal experience with this command is that it is the hardest to teach and takes the longest for your dog to learn. When I say it is the hardest command to teach it is not because of the difficulties of putting your dog into this command or that it is labor intensive. I say it is the hardest command to teach because if what a dog has to go through to accept doing this command for you. Down is the most submissive command you will ask your dog to do as an obedience command. Every dog will resist this command one way or another.

Every dog does resist this command when it is taught correctly. Because dogs live in a hierarchy, they will test the boundaries to test their level in the hierarchy. It is in their nature to do so. When the Down command is taught appropriately, you take a role with your dog that lets her know she does not need (or cannot) to continue to test for a higher level in the pack. Once a dog knows and accepts their place in the pack, she can then get on with her life and will accept the role she is to play for the rest of her life. When put into those terms, you can see why it is so important for you to teach your dog to do the Down command willingly.

The happiest dogs I see are the dogs that have accepted this role and no longer have to vie for pack leadership or to even try to dominate any person or any other dog. This means that if you get another dog, there will be a time the two dogs have to figure out where they are with each other. But, if you are taking the leadership role you need, both dogs will go through that process and you may never see it because it is easier for them.

The most important thing you need to know about the Down command is that your dog has to do the command willingly. If your dog does the command while expecting something from you, it is not being done willingly. If your dog does the command out of fear, she will, at some point, continue to test the boundaries. Many behaviors go away when an owner teaches their dog to do a down and their dog does the down willingly.

Discussion Points:
1) When teaching the Down command what are you using to get your dog to lie down for the first time?
2) How would you know if your dog is doing the Down command willingly?

- **All dogs must go through resistance while learning the Down command. This command must be done willingly in order for your dog to accept its place under you in the hierarchy. The Down command is the most submissive command you will ask of your dog.**

Lying down willingly is the breakthrough you need in order to work on any behaviors or habits you would like to eliminate. If the Down command is not done willingly, you will not be able to get the long-lasting results you desire. As mentioned above, this command is the most important command and the one your dog will resist the most. Does it not seem logical that if your dog has such a tough time with doing this command for you that she will resist doing the command? To me, yes.

There are many thing dogs do when resisting doing a down for an owner. I have seen everything from trying to run away to just locking their legs and pushing against being put into the down position. I have even seen dogs that have never shown signs of aggression get aggressive toward an owner when teaching this command. It is very rare that it takes less than three weeks to get a dog to do this command on its own. Usually you, the owner, do not do enough downs with your dog. Because of this you will see negative results later in other ways.

A big reason dogs resist this command is lack of trust. If your dog does not trust you, it is usually because you have been very inconsistent with your communication and expectations of your dog. When you are inconsistent, your dog does not know when or how things must be in your family. You have not done your part to create that trust.

If you went into your job every day not knowing what mood your boss was going to be in or whether or not you were going to have a job when you got there, it would be miserable. I have heard it called, 'Walking on egg shells.' If your dog has this same feeling around you because you have not established the rules (created structure), then she definitely will not want to show submission toward you unless out of fear.

Discussion Points:
1) Are you willing to work through your dog's resistance to get a down willingly? If so, what would that look like for you and your dog?
2) Have you built trust from your dog by being consistent in your expectations?

- **The key to understanding most commands is to have your dog hold that command for longer periods of time with bigger distractions.**

This is especially true for the down commands, Down and Place. To hold these commands for a long period helps to reinforce these two commands because they are submissive commands to your dog. As we discussed in the above command postulates, Down is the most submissive command you will give your dog. All dogs resist the Down command, and it must be done willingly.

This also works with the Sit command, only as long as your dog knows she is in a command. In other words, you have to reinforce that your dog is holding whatever command you gave. How does your dog know she is in a command? You have to add distraction. If your dog breaks the command you gave, you have to stay on task and put her back into that command.

It is important that you still abide by the **Rules of Distraction**, the **Three Corrections Rule**, and the **Rule of No** when practicing this postulate. It can be very frustrating to get your dog to hold a command she has just learned. It is also best that you build on the time. Start with a small amount of time (five seconds) then build to more substantial amounts of time. For a Sit command, three minutes is a significant amount of time. For the Down command, five to 10 minutes is a good target, although a dog should be able to hold this command (and the Place command) for well above 30 minutes, if necessary.

Once you build up to the longer times, it is up to you to pay attention and be aware if your dog has broken the command. If you don't catch that your dog broke the command within five seconds, you have lost your corrective opportunity.

Discussion Points:
1) Why does holding a command help a dog learn a command?
2) When does a dog know the difference between holding a command for you and just being in that position?

- **The Place command is a confidence-building command for your dog. For your dog to hold a command while you do other things helps your dog learn to do for you, even when you are not giving her direct attention.**

The Place command serves several purposes. The Place command starts the process of teaching your dog more advanced commands and obedience. It also starts your dog on the path of learning to make decisions on her own. You also start the off-leash process because you will be dropping the leash and expecting your dog to still work for you.

First, the Place command is a target command. "Place" means your dog goes to a target, the mat, and lies down on it. Teaching your dog to go to a target is the first step to teaching many other target commands. In the excellence level of obedience trials, a dog has to pick out a shape, retrieve it, and bring it back to the owner. There are other target commands you could teach as well. You could name each of your dog's toys, you could teach your dog to go to her crate or her bed, or you could teach her who is who in your home and have her go to that person.

Second, the Place command is a multilayered command. It takes two steps to train your dog on this command. First, you have to teach her to lie down on the mat, then you have to teach her to walk to the mat on her own and lie down. This taught me that if I could break down a command into small enough parts, I could teach my dog anything. I once had a client that taught his dog "Bang." When he stood facing the dog, he would put his hand in his pocket, pull out his hand, point at the dog and say "Bang." The dog would then roll over, as if shot, and play dead. By breaking any command, or trick, down into small enough parts, it makes it manageable to the point that when you put it all together, it looks like one command or trick.

Another purpose, and what I feel is the most important reason to teach this command, is that it is a confidence-builder for your dog. Most dogs I work with lack self-confidence. Fear and anxiety are the most common reasons for aggression. Both are a lack of self-confidence and a lack of good communication from both the owner and the dog. The Place command helps to increase this self-confidence and communication when done appropriately.

For a dog that has a lot of self-confidence, this command is also a benefit. For the confident dog, the Place command teaches them to make decisions on their own. When your dog knows its place in your pack, she will begin to take her role with confidence. She makes decisions based on what she knows you want her to do even when you are not around. This is very evident when an owner and dog have great communication and a great bond.

Discussion Points:
1) Where and how do you think you would break up this command to teach the separate parts?
2) Is your dog a confident dog or does your dog lack self-confidence?

- **It is in your dog's nature to test the boundaries. The more structure you create and the more consistent you are, the less your dog will test the boundaries you have established.**

Overlapping with the "Dominance is about trust" postulate, this goes more in-depth about why your dog continues to do the behaviors that drive you crazy.

It is *not* in her nature to pee outside. It is in her nature to pee wherever and whenever she needs to pee. It is also in her nature to mark her territory. It is *not* in your dog's nature to sit and lie down when told. It is in her nature to sit and lie down when she is tired or wants to watch something.

Just because you have these expectations of your dog does not mean your dog will just comply and want to do these things. In human nature, you think you can explain something once or twice and others (children, dogs, family, or colleagues) should comply. This is a big problem in communication.

Your dog is a dog. She thinks like a dog and learns like a dog. It is up to you to change how *you* communicate to teach and train your dog. When you try to set boundaries (make rules for your dog), you will see that she will do many things to keep you from doing your job. Why? Because it is your dog's nature. Dog's naturally just want to eat, sleep, and poop. Anything else you expect your dog to do is outside of those basic needs.

I say it is your dog's job to test the boundaries. If you look at it as your dog's job, then you will be expecting the tests. Knowing that your dog is going to test the boundaries is the first step to getting better at training. When you understand that your dog is going to test the boundaries, then you will be ready for the tests. This is when I ask an owner, "Who is being distracted? You or the dog?"

In typical training sessions, you expect your dog to comply with every command, hand sign, motivation, or correction you give. Because of this, when your dog does something different, you panic. Corrections become over-the-top, motivation goes out the window, and your praise is non-existent.

Discussion Points:
1) Who is being distracted? You or your dog?
2) "It is your dog's *job* to test the boundaries." What is the meaning of this statement?

- **A dog does not truly know a command until she has done that command over 1,000 times on her own, with no prompting (motivation or correction) from the owner.**

This postulate goes along with the **Ten to One Rule** I teach. Also, if you have not noticed already, I do many things in threes. If you have to praise 10 times for every one correction, you need to be putting your dog into situations over and over again. You also have to keep up with the number of times you correct, use distractions, put your dog into a command or situation, or motivate.

$$10 \times 10 \times 10 = 1,000 \text{ [Three tens]}$$

Your dog needs massive repetition to really understand, or learn, something. The only way a dog learns is through praise or positive reinforcement. Because of this, your dog needs to have one of two things to learn: many, many, many, many, many, many, many, repetitions or a *major* action or reaction to a behavior.

Repetition is a key ingredient for you and your dog to learn expected behavior. Many times, when an owner thinks they have done as much of a command as they need to do, I give the same homework I gave the week prior because I see that the dog has not really learned a behavior or a command. As an owner, it is tough to see this because you are bored with the repetition or you are just so pleased to finally see results that you are willing to move on after the slightest accomplishment.

If a major action or reaction happens, a dog is more than likely to remember that event and act accordingly. In other words, your dog has learned to act a certain way in a certain situation. A good example is the vacuum cleaner. The first time you bring out this machine out and turn it on, it may freak your dog out. From that moment on, if you do not work on desensitizing your dog to the vacuum cleaner, your dog will always show fear of it.

This is also why I have the rule that you must praise your dog in a bigger way than you corrected. If you can create a major positive reaction, then you can get your dog to remember to act certain ways in certain situations. This is why treat training is such a popular method of training. For a highly food-motivated dog, getting a treat when doing a command is a highly positive result for doing whatever command was asked.

Discussion Points:
1) Why 1,000 times? What is the significance in that number?
2) What two ways do dogs remember certain things?

- **When you have a great attitude, no matter what the situation, you will always see better results because you are looking for and expecting better results.**

Attitude is everything. Attitude creates your outlook on how you approach your family, your job, and your dog. When you can recognize this and make adjustments to your attitude prior to training your dog, you can and will have great results. You will be looking for great results.

Are you on 'Cloud Nine' or 'Down in the Dumps'? Your outlook on what is around you will be determined by either of these feelings. Are you coming home and looking for all the bad things your dog did while you were gone? Or, maybe you just can't wait to get home to that loving, fun dog you got as a companion? The world you see around you, what you expect to see, and how you determine how things are going are all based on the attitude and feelings you have in the moment and you get to choose.

I have a sign above my front door that says, "The happiest people don't have the best of everything, they just make the best of everything." To me this is about looking for and expecting great results. Even if the results are small, they will be noticed with this attitude. I think a big problem with dog training is that most people want big results fast. Most people don't want to do the work and yet have a great dog. I feel this is why there is still such a disposable outlook when it comes to a family pet and why the shelters are overrun with all types of pets.

If you knew you had to keep a dog for life when you bought it, you would make better choices and be more educated before committing to a pet. Most of you that bought this book don't have that attitude and for that I am grateful. Many of you have problems and know that something can be done to fix the problems with your dog. Many of you are not willing to give your dog up. This simple change in attitude is what will get you through the problems and get you to a place where you have an amazing family member instead of just a dog.

Discussion Points:
1) What can you do to change your attitude when you notice you are frustrated or angry with your dog?
2) Why do you think your attitude is a factor when working with your dog?

- **Body language is the number one way your dog learns from you. Your body language can change the mood, choice, or direction of your dog without you even knowing it. When using hand signals along with obedience commands, your dog will learn that command much quicker.**

In the past, I have taught and worked on competitive training with dogs. During this time, one great lesson I learned was how my body language is so important to my dog. When you work with your dog and are expecting one thing, but your dog keeps doing another, the first thing you should look at is your body language. Your body language can be saying something very different from what your mouth is saying.

There were times my daughter's dog, Gabby, and I were running the agility course, and I would verbally give one command, such as "jump," and she would run through the tunnel. What I learned was that my body language was saying "tunnel," not "jump." I would be facing toward the tunnel and even when I pointed to the jump, it looked to her like I was pointing to the tunnel. I had to become very aware of the direction I wanted Gabby to take by making sure my motion, body angle, and the direction I was pointing were overly exaggerated toward the obstacle I wanted her to go to next.

This was a big lesson for me in many ways. When I train a new client, especially with children, I show them all the commands in a very over-exaggerated way. Most adults will not mimic this because it looks ridiculous, but their children will. I learned this from my daughter as well. She would do almost all of the commands with a very animated way of doing each of the signs for each of the commands. Her dog, Gabby, really picked up on things with her and would respond to her more quickly than with me.

When I started training Molly, she would not stay on her place mat when I gave her the command. I would start to walk toward her, give her the command again, and she would look up at me before totally ignoring what I said to go on with what she was doing. This infuriated me. I would stomp toward her and she would run!

I was taught to correct her all the way back to her place mat, so I would get worked up that she was not doing what I told her to do, and I would go after her in an angry fashion. When she saw this body language, she would run away and I would give chase. After many times of doing this and getting nowhere with the Place command, I finally caught her, and decided I was done chasing her. I took off her collar, sat down, and had a discussion. I told her if she wanted to be with me, she had to want to stay with me. I gave her big love and then got up and headed home, tired, frustrated, and refusing to chase her any more. She followed me.

For the most part, she followed me all the way home. Every now and then, I would stop, give her more big-love, tell her that I wanted her to be my dog, and then again start home. She continued to follow, and every time I stopped to give her attention, she did not shy away or show signs of fearing me. This was the beginning of how I understood to train dogs and how body language plays such a big part in training your dog. I definitely did not realize it in the moment, but it was the shift I needed to make to get to where I am now with training.

Discussion Points:
1) Why do you think body language is so key in a dog's ability to learn from you?
2) Can you think of a time when your dog reacted differently than what you expected? Do you think it could have been because of your body language?

- **Dogs pick up on your body language before they pick up on any other mode of communication from you. It usually takes a dog about six months to learn and really understand your body language.**

This is what I tell all new dog owners. Why is this introductory period important? Whenever you get a dog, that dog has already learned certain social skills. They learned these skills from their litter-mates and parents or, if you got an older dog, they have learned to live in a different environment than yours. The social skills they learned may be very different than what you expect from your new dog. Because of this, they must adapt to their new environment, just as you are adapting to the new dog and teaching new skills.

During this introductory period, your dog is learning from you the best way she can, through your body language. Your body language lets her know when you are serious and when you are not. Have you ever seen your dog react differently to you when you approach her on several different occasions? You may not think you are approaching any differently, yet your dog is enthused to greet you one time, then another time your dog cowers or shies away. This is because your body language is sending a different message.

The reasons for the different reaction could be because of your mood or your energy. As an owner, you don't think of these things in everyday interactions with your dog, yet your dog does. This is the main way she communicates with you, and the small changes that go on with you and your body language are picked up by her. During the first few months she is with you, she is learning to recognize how you behave with each movement you make.

Recognize that you create volumes of communication with your dog just by being around her. It can help you in those moments of frustration when you do not know why your dog is doing or reacting in a certain way. In the Discover Your Dog Podcast, episode 005, I give homework that hopefully would reveal how your dog interprets your body language.

Discussion Points:
1) If your mood or energy affect your body language, what can you do to effectively communicate with your dog?
2) Can you change your body language so that you are sending your dog an appropriate message?

- **When leash training, leaving the leash on your dog creates a sense of control whether you are touching the leash or not.**

By using a leash, you have physical control and the ability to make your dog choose to do what you want her to do. With this style of training, you also create a dependency on the leash. Your dog will quickly understand the significance of the leash. In a first-time training situation, whenever an owner gets the leash for the lesson, the dog will almost always go for the door. Why? Because previously the leash was only used for going outside.

When you have been working with your dog on-leash for a certain amount of time, you may notice that your dog behaves differently when off the leash compared to on-leash. Again, you are in physical control, and you are really only working on behaviors while on-leash. Your dog has started to relate behaving to the leash, not you.

This is why it is good to leave the leash on your dog when you are working on specific behaviors. Because your dog has connected the leash with behaving and making good choices (if you have been doing your training well), by leaving the leash on her you are giving her an opportunity to make those better choices. You get the opportunity to praise her in the moment for making the choice you want.

Most people relate the leash to being in control or in charge. The reality is you only have physical control. If you overuse the leash, then the *only* time your dog will behave is when she is on the leash. The leash is only part of the process of teaching your dog that she can make choices on her own. I compare it to freestyle rock climbing. At first, you use the harness and ropes until you build up the strength and confidence that you can climb the cliff.

Discussion Points:
1) Why is it important to have the leash on in the first place?
2) What is the significance of the leash in the process toward training off-leash?

- **Correcting your dog long after a behavior you don't want, or away from the location of the infraction, does not make sense to her. That correction has nothing to do with the past behavior and your dog thinks what she is doing at the time of the correction is why she is getting corrected. You have about a five-second reaction time once you see a behavior you want to correct. Any amount of time beyond that is too late.**

Timeliness is very significant in dog training. I am impeccable with my timing on a correction, with my praise, and with when and how much motivation to use. I have seen shows where the trainers are impeccable with their timing as well. Unfortunately, this takes practice.

Why are we so good with our timing? Because we have reached a point, after training thousands of dogs and owners, where we know when something is more likely to happen. Not only that, but many times, I see that a dog is about to do something before an owner sees it. I see a dog's body language and I know what is coming next.

The trick is to wait on the action, then react to that action appropriately. As you are learning to communicate with your dog, you will start to see these signs as well. Typically, you will anticipate something instead of waiting for it to happen, and you will act inappropriately.

A good example is when I am teaching an owner to teach their dog the Down command. After a few weeks of watching their dog, I see the signs that tell me their dog is ready to lie down. I always like for the owner to get the first down, so I will stop working with the dog and give the leash to the owner. Once I describe what to do, the owner will follow the instructions (usually the same things they have been doing for the past three weeks) and give the Down command. While I am watching, the dog will start to lie down and the owner freaks out and jerks on the leash. What the owner just did was to anticipate that the dog was going to get up or walk away, not lie down.

The owner was not used to seeing their dog go through process of completing the down command. They were used to seeing the dog resist the command. That past experience created the anticipation and inappropriate reaction. Most of the time, if I was not there to point it out, they would keep doing the same thing, and the mixed message would make the dog even more resistant to that command.

When I am training a person with their dog, one problem I run into is that the owner gets into a hurry. Phrases become lumped together, body language is thrown out of whack, and voice tones are inappropriate. You have five seconds to respond to whatever type of behavior you are working on. Five seconds is a long time in dog training, and for your dog, it is about how long it takes for her brain to move on to something else.

By taking five seconds, you also have time to assess the situation. What type of behavior is it? How strong of a reaction do you need to take? Is it something that can be ignored? It took you less than five seconds just to read those three questions, and by taking your time, you are giving your dog a chance to make a choice. If you tell your dog to sit and she does not, by getting impatient you may not give her a chance to react to your command. You then will be giving attention to something you don't want, standing.

You do not have to wait five seconds every time. You just need to be aware of when you are overreacting or getting in a hurry, compared to being impeccable with the timing of your reaction. Sometimes a quick praise in the moment is the best reaction.

Discussion Points:
1) Why do you have five seconds to react to your dog's behavior?
2) How do you know you have waited too long or reacted too quickly?

- **Looking your dog in the eyes is one of two things: praise or a challenge. As an owner, you are never challenging your dog, ever. To look your dog in her eyes at the moment she is doing anything is praising her for that thing.**

Eye contact is a form of praise. Really, it is only a form of praise if you are making that eye contact with your own dog. If you are making eye contact with a strange dog, it then can be a challenge. I teach this when training an owner.

Your dog learns things about you through your body language and voice tone. Because of this knowledge, it is very hard to threaten your own dog. This means that, for you, eye contact is mainly praise. You are rarely, if ever, challenging your dog by making eye contact with her.

While training your dog, you have to be aware of when you give eye contact. For example, if you tell your dog to lie down, and she sits there staring at you with you staring back at her, you are praising her for sitting, even though you gave the Down command. The best thing to do is look away, as if to say "I am not giving you attention until you do what I say." It is even appropriate to cross your arms or turn you back on her. All of these actions are body language that tell your dog she is not doing what you asked of her.

Sometimes your dog will do the same to you. Many times, I have seen a dog totally shun its owner when she was in a situation she did not like. Dogs will look away or even huff. It is their way of telling you they do not want to do whatever you have asked them to do.

Discussion Points:
1) Many times people use eye contact to get their point across. Does this work for dogs?
2) Can dogs use eye contact to their advantage?

- **Control is about confidence. Confidence comes from knowing what you are communicating in every given situation. Once you are aware of your communication, you are going to naturally be consistent.**

This postulate can be very confusing, since it seems incongruent with some of the others. The confusing part is that you may think you are very confident about working and training your dog, but what you think is confidence is a feeling rather than knowledge. Just because you are confident about how you handle yourself does not mean you are doing it appropriately. When you are communicating appropriately with your dog, then you don't have to worry about consistency. Why? Because you are working with your dog in proper ways, and you are looking for good behaviors and reactions instead of reacting to bad behaviors.

When you are communicating appropriately you never have to worry about being consistent, because appropriate communication will always be consistent. In other words, if you know, in every given situation, what you are communicating, you never have to worry about being consistent. Why? Because on the rare times you go off course or communicate in a way you didn't want, you will catch it and correct it immediately. Anything you do once or twice does not create or correct a behavior.

This is the type of control I am talking about. Control is not about being in charge or being the dominant. It is about confidently communicating through appropriate means. It is about knowing what you want, and communicating that appropriately, no matter the situation. Most of the time, especially with a confident and controlling dog, you won't even realize you are communicating in this manner.

When I ask an owner what it means to be in control, most of the time they tell me it means they are in charge. Being in control is really about knowing what you want, then going for it. You do what you want, when you want, and how you want. Most people that I consider "in control" of their lives live like this without even thinking about it.

Example: You and a friend travel to a new and unfamiliar city together. This is the first time you have travelled together, and you are excited. One night, you tell your friend that you have made reservations at a local restaurant, and you would like to go out after dinner for drinks or dancing. Your friend does not seem so enthused so you tell him you will pay for dinner. He agrees. When it is time to go, he is not ready, and you even have to get a little stern with him to get him out the door. You are late for your reservations, but they still let you in. Your friend is not impressed with the place, yet he is polite and stays through the dinner. You tell him to pick the place to go out afterwards and give him some options of things you found. He says he would rather just "wing it" and see what happens and picks a place to start.

After dinner, you both leave and taxi it to the first spot. After the first drink, your friend says he is bored and wants to try a new place. You tell him to give it a chance and buy him another drink. After a moment, you get up to go to the bathroom and when you come back, your friend is gone, half his drink is still at the bar, and the bartender tells you he paid the tab.

In this example, it is easy to see who was in charge, right? Your friend. But, can you name every situation in which he took charge of the situation? Obviously, your friend is a jerk and you were in charge. You made the reservations, got him moving, picked the places to go, and even threatened to get a new hotel when he disappeared on you. You're in charge, right? Wrong.

Just the fact that you had to convince your friend to go to the restaurant, then get angry at him to get him moving started the process of him being in control. Then, he went to the bar with you after and left when he wanted. You had to bribe, beg, and scream, and he still did what he wanted. Your friend probably had no intentions of hurting you, he just knew what he wanted to do, and he did it without thinking. He probably thought you would just hang out at the bar because it was what you wanted to do. His confidence and control were not conscious.

This is why "Control is about Confidence."

Discussion Points:
1) What is control?
2) How is this revealed in our personal lives?

- **Humans have personalities. Because of this, you will find that different people react very differently in many situations. This includes members of the same family as well as people of different sexes, ages, races, and personal backgrounds.**

Humans have personalities. When mixing with each other (humans), it is hard enough to understand the personality of the person you are with, let alone the dog you bring into the family. Because humans have such a tough time understanding and accepting the fact that others have differing personalities, it can make for a difficult situation. Dating, marriage, social and business functions, or just keeping to yourself—these social situations call for taking a look at the differing personalities and finding a way to function.

Once you understand the personality of your dog, it is best to adjust your training and interactions to your dog's personality rather than trying to adjust your dog's personality. Changing your personality or your dog's personality is almost impossible and can be very detrimental. To change a personality of a dog is to "break" the dog.

When you do recognize that dogs do have personalities, and you can adjust your behavior toward your dog, you will be well on your way to having a happy and well-fused family. Working with your dog instead of against your dog is always a better choice and makes for a comfortable, stable environment. It is up to you to have this awareness and willingness to work through the differences in each of your personalities because your dog cannot.

Discussion Points:
1) How do you know if you are picking a dog that has a personality that will be compatible to your personality?
2) If there is a huge gap in the owner's and the dog's personality, can it be overcome?

- **Dogs have personalities. Because of this, you will find that different dogs react very different in many situations. This includes dogs of the same breed.**

I do believe that dogs have personalities. I have even told owners in the past that it is very difficult to change a dog's personality. To change a dog's personality would be to break it. Typically, the only time an owner would want this is if the dog was very dominant or aggressive. It is very rare that a dog is a true dominant-aggressive; I believe it's about 0.3%. (Three out of every 1,000 dogs.)

I get many calls because an owner bought the same breed of dog they had before and the new dog is "so different" than the last dog. Most people would not get the same breed of dog if it was wild or hard to handle the first time. Mainly because you think that breed will be the same with every dog.

It is true that a certain breed of dog will keep certain traits, but just because the dog is the same breed does not mean it will have the same personality. For example, I know that almost every Beagle I work with is going be stubborn, and yet I have worked with some that are very outgoing, some that are mild mannered, and even some that were very aggressive. They were all still stubborn and knowing this helps me to explain to an owner the difficulties they will go through when training.

Discussion Points:
1) How can you recognize your dog's personality?
2) Even if you know a dog's base traits, is that going to predict that dog's personality? Why are these two things different?

- **If there is a behavior you are okay with in general, but would like your dog to stop doing when told, correct with a word or phrase then immediately praise her for doing what you asked. This shows her it was okay to do that thing, but she should stop when told.**

While specifically training for behavior I came across three types of behaviors.

1. A behavior you never want to happen.
2. A behavior you are okay with; you just want it to stop when told.
3. A behavior you want.

An example of number two is barking at the door when someone knocks. If you have a dog, more than likely you are okay with a few barks at the door to let someone know you have a dog. If this is the case, more than likely you don't want your dog to continue barking while you are trying to have a conversation with the person you just let into your home. This is a behavior you are okay with when it happens, but you want the behavior to stop when you tell your dog to stop.

For this type of behavior, you have to use a word or phrase as the correction to get your dog to stop doing what she is doing and pay attention. If your dog stops the behavior, you then immediately praise your dog. Immediately praising after the corrective word teaches your dog that it was okay to do that thing; she just needs to stop when told.

This is very different than number one, the behavior you don't want. For a behavior you don't want, you use the corrective word

"No," then give no attention when your dog stops doing the behavior and pays attention to you.

This is also why I teach an owner to use a corrective word or phrase when correcting for a behavior you just want your dog to stop at the time. Using a word or phrase for a correction differentiates which type of behavior it is.

One of the most common mistakes I see is that you immediately praise your dog when she quits a behavior you don't want. This happens a lot when a dog is jumping up. Owners say things like, "off," "down," or any combination of those two words, and then the owner might pet the dog to calm her down. Without realizing it, that owner is using praise and teaching their dog to continue doing that behavior.

Discussion Points:
1) What are the three types of behaviors and how are they different?
2) How do you know if the behavior is: one you want, one you don't ever want, or one you are okay with as long as she stops when told?

Acknowledgements

My first thought goes to isa, The Institute for Self-Actualization. Since 2008 I have mentors, friends, and family because of the process of learning to believe in the most important person...Me. Because of the lessons I learned in isa I have run multiple businesses with people that I trust. Also, because of isa, the Goals Group was formed. It has been the sole push to most of the accomplishments and relationships I have manifested in my life.

To the FDF Group: Devin, Leslie, Karissa, and Whitney you are why this book is here and why Family Dog Fusion exists. Your belief in me has propelled my desire to spread the word and continue the process of teaching others to enjoy their dogs. The podcasts are an integral part of what we do. The podcasts, and you, are why this book is going to be a huge success!

Kate and Jessica, thank you for starting me on this path and being supportive to my whims throughout our time together. I put you through a lot and you both are amazing in spite of me.

Shanda and Tim, thank you both for taking the time to edit this book. Shanda your ideas and opinions of my book, even though daunting, were what I needed to get this process started.

To the dogs that taught me everything, tested my boundaries, and showed me that communication and an intense bond with a domesticated dog is truly possible; Gabby, Molly, and Oz. I will love and remember you always.

And to my biggest fan, Tam, thank you for putting up with my shitty personality. You have endured with me through this entire process and have always been my rock. You are my best friend! I love you.

Made in the USA
Coppell, TX
27 October 2019